THE WORLD OF
BIBLICAL LITERATURE

BOOKS BY ROBERT ALTER

Rogue's Progress: Studies in the Picaresque Novel

Fielding and the Nature of the Novel

After the Tradition

Modern Hebrew Literature

Partial Magic: The Novel as a Self-Conscious Genre

Defenses of the Imagination

A Lion for Love: A Critical Biography of Stendhal

The Art of Biblical Narrative

Motives for Fiction

The Art of Biblical Poetry

The Invention of Hebrew Prose

The Literary Guide to the Bible
(co-edited with Frank Kermode)

The Pleasures of Reading in an Ideological Age

Necessary Angels

THE WORLD OF
BIBLICAL
LITERATURE

Robert Alter

BasicBooks
A Division of HarperCollins*Publishers*

Library of Congress Cataloging-in-Publication Data

Alter, Robert.
    The world of Biblical literature / Robert Alter.
        p.   cm.
    Includes bibliographical references and index.
    ISBN 0–465–09255–1
    1. Bible as literature.   I. Title.
    BS535.A57   1991
    809' .93522—dc20   91–55462
                                                        CIP

For Michael André Bernstein
with affection
some thoughts on the first tale of the tribe

CONTENTS

PREFACE

My two earlier books on the Bible, *The Art of Biblical Narrative* (1981) and *The Art of Biblical Poetry* (1985), were attempts to provide analytic, illustrative primers for the two major genres of biblical literature. The third conspicuous mode of writing in the Hebrew Bible, law, may have some purposeful relation to its surrounding narrative contexts, as a couple of recent critics have proposed, but it does not seem to me sufficiently linked in form and aims to our system of literary genres to sustain the kinds of analysis I undertook in my two previous books.

When I was first drawn to work on this subject, in the mid-1970s, the notion that one could understand the Bible in serious, even rigorous, terms as literature was still relatively new, and the attempts to do so, with a few notable exceptions, were rather fumbling. As a result, I may have presented myself, a bit more than was strictly justified, as a voice crying in the wilderness. It is a pleasure to report that since then a vivid spectrum of exciting developments in the literary discussion of the Bible has emerged. Both literary and biblical scholars have made valuable contributions to this new movement, which really seems to be in the process of redefining our relation to the whole body of ancient texts that is one of the two great matrices of our culture. Some of the recent books on this subject apply literary analysis to particular biblical texts; or try to synthesize a literary method with the procedures of historical and text-critical scholarship; or explore the general nature of biblical literature, its distinctive purposes, and what might connect it with or set it off from other and later literatures in the Western tradition. In studying all this new work, I have learned a good deal, and even critics with whom I disagree profoundly, like Northrop Frye and Harold Bloom, have raised certain challenging questions that lead me (and I should think anyone) to reconsider the fundamental assumptions that underlie any possible literary reading of the Bible.

It is to a series of reflections on those assumptions that the present volume is devoted. In keeping with this purpose, I have not included several pieces published as articles in the 1980s that are efforts to deal with unfinished business left over from *The Art of Biblical Narrative*—either elaborations of concepts I developed in that book, like the notion of type-scene, or discussions of topics in the poetics of biblical narrative I had neglected, like the organization of episodes into larger narrative unities. The one chapter here that might also happily have served as a chapter in *The Art of Biblical Narrative*—if I had only been smart enough a decade ago to recognize the paramount importance of intrabiblical allusion for the ancient Hebrew writers—is the chapter on allusion. That discussion, however, seemed to me necessary for the argument of this book as well, because allusion is in my view an essential aspect of the distinctive language of literature and hence a vital consideration in defining the literary character of the Bible.

In most of these essays I move from the particular case to the larger literary context or the larger theoretical issue, or begin with these larger questions and attempt to think about them through an analysis of particular cases. Nearly everything I have written (and not only on the Bible) flows from the conviction that it is not possible in principle to separate metacritical or theoretical reflection from formal analysis. If you want to think about what kind of book, or collection of books, the Bible is; what submerged or explicit unities it might possess; what tacit conceptions of literature informed ancient Hebrew writing; what lines of connection might exist between the literature of ancient Israel and later, secular literatures— you must begin by looking at the formal articulations of the literary texts. The way a writer shapes a scene, reports details, bends language into dialogue, and builds the symmetries of a line of verse and the development of a poetic image tells you a great deal about how he conceives human and divine nature, history, causality, and destiny, and also something about his relation to the literary medium in which all this is worked out.

My concern in this book with the global picture of biblical literature, reinforced by some of the recent invigorating discussions of the nature of the Bible as a literary medium, has led me to contemplate certain underlying questions of definition and conceptualization. In what sense can we, with our fundamentally secular assumptions about literary expression, speak of the Bible as literature? If literature involves a powerful component of imaginative free play, can there be any real place for so anarchic, perhaps even subversive, an impulse in a body of texts as spiritually intent and as ideologically freighted as the Bible? Is there any discernible methodological priority or complementarity between a literary approach and historical or text-critical approaches to the Bible? What is the role of any of these methodologies in a modern commentary? Authors are deeply implicated in our idea of literature, but how are we to talk about authorship in a body of texts where anonymity is the rule and the writer—or the writer assimilated by the editor—blends into the voice of national tradition? What place does this once authoritative corpus have in contemporary culture, and can the attempt to recover the Bible as literature affect whatever that place might be? What do the media of narrative and poetry have to do with the aims and the worldview of the biblical writers?

These are large questions, to which I certainly do not pretend to offer any neat answers. I will be happy if this book succeeds in setting readers to think in a certain direction about how such questions can be confronted. For me as reader and critic, the confrontation, as I have said, almost always involves at some point a close focus of attention on specific texts. I repeatedly do this—as in one way or another I have done in all my books—not only for rhetorical reasons, in order to make my points more vividly accessible to readers, but also for epistemological reasons, because it seems to me that no critical or theoretical generalization is worth its words unless it can be seen to stand the complicating test of the individual instance. This book, then, resembles both *The Art of Biblical Narrative* and *The Art of Biblical Poetry* in the fondness it exhibits for scrutinizing specific textual cases. But whereas this procedure was in my two earlier books conducted with the purpose of defining the formal means of the two major literary genres in the Bible, *The World of Biblical Literature* tries to move from the specific texts to an apprehension of that world of writing, how it turns, how and why it is literary. On such issues there obviously can be no definitive statement. My hope for this book is that it will add a useful voice to the already lively debate about the essential character of these endlessly elusive, endlessly fascinating texts that still nourish our culture.

ACKNOWLEDGMENTS

Chapters 3 and 8 originally appeared in *The Literary Guide to the Bible*, a 1987 book I co-edited with Frank Kermode, and I would like to thank the Harvard University Press for permission to use that material here. Chapters 6, 7, and 9 were originally published as articles in *Commentary* (respectively, March 1990, November 1991, and August 1985), and I want to thank the editors of the magazine for giving me the rights to these essays. Secretarial expenses for this volume were paid for by funds from the Class of 1937 Chair at the University of California at Berkeley. I am grateful to Janet Livingstone for her faithful assistance in preparing the typescript. All translations of the Hebrew Bible are my own. I have often chosen to sacrifice gracefulness or elegance in English usage in order to retain certain features of the original, but I hope the surrounding literary analysis will justify this procedure.

CHAPTER 1

A Peculiar Literature

The new wave of literary studies of the Bible has been gathering momentum now for more than a decade, and it promises to have far-reaching consequences for both biblical and literary scholarship. It is an academic development that may also exert some broader cultural influence, for it can help us, as I argue in detail in chapter 9, to *read* the Bible again, instead of sorting out its components, reconstructing it, and looking for some textual or historical reality that lies behind the text we have. Not surprisingly, however, there is no clear consensus on what the precise object of reading is or on how the reading might most appropriately be undertaken.

Any modern effort to look at the Bible from a literary perspective must grapple with two fundamental difficulties: the peculiar circumstances of the composition and evolution of the biblical text; and the peculiar aims, even the peculiar

objects of representation, toward which the literary art of the
Bible is directed. Let me first try to explain how the issues of
the text confront the literary critic of the Bible with a whole
series of bafflements.

For both the common reader and the critic, the reading of a
work of literature is predicated on an assumption of authorship that goes all the way back to the Greek tragedians and to
Virgil and that for many centuries was retrojected still earlier,
to the constructed authorial figure of Homer. The author, a
person with a distinctive sensibility and a distinctive freight
of experience, puts a personal stamp on the work, however
"mediated," contradictory, or ventriloquistically disguised its
formal embodiment may be. A French-inspired vogue in literary theory sought for a while to displace the living author
with a notion of the text as a playground of impersonal literary codes, but that view seems increasingly one-sided, and the
assumption of ordinary readers about an informing authorial
presence is confirmed in the practice of most critics, even at
this postmodern moment. The author addresses us with a representation of or reflection on life spun out of the densely tan-
gled stuff of his own lived life, and thus the act of reading is a
kind of colloquy—the author speaking, the reader thinking
back—between him and us. Authorship is also the implicit
guarantee of the unity of the literary work. Joyce's *Ulysses*
may leap and slide from third-person omniscience to stream
of consciousness, mock-epic, and surreal drama, but as readers, even without a theory of the novel's architectonic unity,
we know it is emphatically, extravagantly Joycean from
beginning to end.[1]

The case is quite different with the Bible, and this has cost
all of us would-be literary analysts of the Bible a good deal of
perplexity. Biblical tradition itself went to great lengths to
hide the tracks of the individual author. There is no proclama-
tion of authorship, no notion of literary contests as among the

Greeks, no hint of any individual writer aspiring to eternal fame through literary achievement (a recurrent topos and governing idea of Western literature). Instead, the writer disappears into the tradition, makes its voice his, or vice versa. In fact, one of our methodological quandaries is that there is no certain means to determine which of these last two alternatives is the predominant one: did the writer have at his disposal an abundance of precisely formulated narrative materials, perhaps orally transmitted, which he synthesized, or did he fashion his verbal artifact from the mere hints of narrative tradition, in a style that arrogated to itself the authority of hoary national memory and divine knowledge? There is no happy way to remove this cloak of traditional or traditionalizing anonymity. Although scholarly analysis has detected a variety of ideological viewpoints in the text and has sought to link these with various social groups and geographical and temporal settings, the fact of the matter is that all such linkages are grounded in conjecture, with the debates on the dating of particular writers or schools contending over centuries, not decades.

The anonymity of the biblical writer and the absence of context for him are enormously complicated by the intricate process of editing through which his work has come down to us. As with any ancient text, local puzzlements abound— scribal glosses, other kinds of brief interpolations, errors in transcription, and at times wholesale scrambling of passages. But what is far graver for the literary critic is that the stories as a rule appear to have been patched together from disparate and perhaps even conflicting literary sources. The process would be somewhat different for different parts of the Bible (with the first four books of the Pentateuch constituting a distinctive entity; see page 215–16), but in broad outline it would look like this: Two or more literary versions of the same set of events circulated in ancient Israel, let us say, in the early centuries of the Davidic monarchy. An editor chose to make one of these dominant but preserved bits and pieces of one or more competing versions and added his own editorial framework and occasional interventions. Still later, probably early in the period of the return from Babylonian exile, a redactor gave final shape to the text, introducing local modifications of wording, adding some editorial framing and bridging, perhaps winnowing out certain materials, perhaps even incorporating bits of old traditions that had not hitherto been part of the text. All this suggests that the story of King David, even if he is one of the great characters of narrative literature, is built on a textual matrix utterly unlike that of any of the later major narratives in the West, where one master hand has shaped the tale from beginning to end.

What is a literary reader of the Bible to make of this morass? One occasionally hears the accusation that the new literary criticism of the Bible represents, not creedally but methodologically, a new fundamentalism: every element of the text is assumed to be integrally linked with every other, and artistically justified. I can think of no contemporary literary critic of the Bible whose work conforms to this description as a matter of principle, though a few may seem at times to confirm it in their critical practice. All of these critics, that is, recognize that there are problems with the received texts, sometimes requiring emendation or other solutions, and that the sundry hypotheses of a composite text are not to be casually dismissed.

Their analysis, however, has repeatedly argued for a surprising degree of artful coherence in the final version of the text—which in historical terms comes down to an argument for the art of the redactor or for that of a powerfully integrative writer using earlier sources whose work the redactor merely polished. If the proponents of what might be called redactorial integralism sometimes display excessive ingenuity in saving the artistic unity of the text, they nevertheless compel one—especially if one has been trained as a biblical scholar—to read the Bible in a new way because their results are often so good. Works like J. P. Fokkelman's *Narrative Art and Poetry in the Books of Samuel*, Robert Polzin's *Samuel and the Deuteronomist*, and Meir Sternberg's *The Poetics of Biblical Narrative* (which contains some of the most brilliant close readings anyone has done) demonstrate in case after case that there is far more that nicely dovetails or complexly interacts in the elements of the received text than has been imagined in the last two centuries of biblical scholarship.

An opposite strategy from that of the redactorial integralists is to build literary readings on the conclusions of the source criticism that has long dominated biblical studies. That is, if the received text, in its authorless, traditional, and actually composite character, resists the modern critic's need for an individual literary imagination with which to grapple, an author can be rescued from the tangle of the text by association with one of the constituent strands or layers or documents identified by scholarship. The strand designated J or E or P, or the Deuteronomist, or the so-called Court Historian of 1 and 2 Samuel, may thus be assigned an individual sensibility, a gender, an artistic and political agenda, and, if the critic is so inclined, a historical and social location.

The most sensationalistic application of this method is Harold Bloom's in *The Book of J*. An inventive, less flamboyant reading of J and E as authors, using similar notions of authorship, is conducted by Leslie Brisman, a Yale colleague of Bloom's, in *The Voice of Jacob: On the Composition of Genesis*. Although the authorial critics have the virtue of forcing us to rethink conventional assumptions about the Bible, their project is fraught with methodological quandaries on a scale that makes the excesses of redactorial integralism seem relatively minor (see chapter 7). It is questionable whether any one of the strands of the biblical text is really a unitary literary artifact, reflecting a single author and a single moment in time. The difficulties, moreover, in distinguishing between one strand and another on subtle literary grounds like style and sensibility are formidable; they have even led some biblical scholars to wonder whether there actually is an independent E source in the Tetrateuch. And even if one could confidently assume that the hand of an individual author has been identified, all that remains of his—or, for Bloom, her—literary handiwork is not an integral text but the sundry long and short fragments split and spliced and spackled together by the redactor.

David Damrosch, in *The Narrative Covenant*, a thoughtful book that tries both to place biblical narrative in the context of ancient Near Eastern literary history and to keep in view the composite nature of the text, proposes a third way. It is a way with which I partly concur in principle, though sometimes finding myself in disagreement with the implementation of the principle. Damrosch suggests as an apt Oriental analogy for the Bible the *Thousand and One Nights*, a work embodying multiple perspectives that "gives the fullest example of a multifaceted composite artistry produced through a gradual growth of the text." Although the term *composite artistry* is taken from me, Damrosch argues that the choice I spelled out in *The Art of Biblical Narrative*—between a "confused textual patchwork" uncovered by historical criticism and the "purposeful pattern" traced by literary criticism—is a false one. His own project is "the integration of literary and historical study," and what that reveals is rather

> what might be called a purposeful patchwork, though the image lacks enough dimensions, since several different patchworks are variously interlaced and overlaid. In reconstructing this four-dimensional pattern, we read both with and against the intentions of the various authors involved in the text, and

we are also brought to multiple readings of individual passages. To do full justice to the dynamics of biblical narrative, we must often read a passage three or even four ways at once.[2]

As a revision of my own formulation, I quite like Damrosch's Baroque image of multidimensional purposeful patchworks. It admirably preserves the sense of the bumpiness of the biblical text, its repeated use of disparate materials, which should be apparent to any careful analyst working with the original Hebrew. (The redactorial integralists, by contrast, tend to speak of the text as though it were a seamless unity, though at least theoretically they know it is not.) There are, however, two points on which I differ with Damrosch. Suspicious of unjustified harmonizing, he sees—perhaps with the horizon of deconstruction in his peripheral vision—the text as an amalgam of conflicting voices. I would concede that this is sometimes so, but I am also repeatedly impressed by the evidence in many instances of a strong synthesizing imagination that has succeeded in making once disparate voices elements of a complex, persuasively integrated literary whole. In this regard, both the broad structural features and the fine literary articulations of the text often compel me to side with the champions of the redactor's art. The other problem for me in Damrosch's approach is that a literary criticism that seeks to take into account "the various authors involved in the text" must be able to discriminate those authors with some confidence, and I would argue that this is often more difficult to do than Damrosch assumes. His book abounds in astute analysis, but sometimes he sees three sources in a bibilical story where I see two or only one, and where no doubt some more philologically oriented scholars might well discover four or five. Thus, Damrosch's effort to combine literary and historical criticism shares something of the methodological dilemma of the authorial critics.

Gabriel Josipovici, in *The Book of God*, one of the most resonant of the new literary reflections on the Bible, nicely defines
the epistemological quandary that source criticism blithely
evades:

> The inventors of the documentary hypothesis believed that by
> trying to distinguish the various strands they were getting
> closer to *the truth*, which, in good nineteenth-century fashion,
> they assumed to be connected with origins. But in practice the
> contrary seems to have taken place. For their methodology was
> necessarily self-fulfilling: deciding in advance what the Jahwist
> or the Deuteronomist *should* have written, they then called
> whatever did not fit this view an interpolation. But this leads,
> as all good readers know, to the death of reading; for a book
> will never draw me out of myself if I only accept as belonging
> to it what I have already decreed should be there.[3]

The critique of a nineteenth-century bias toward seeking
the truth in origins is particularly shrewd. Whether or not we
join Derrida in assuming that origins are always intrinsically
inaccessible, it is by now clear that when we deal with any
ancient text our approach to origins generally must follow a
risky road of conjecture from the traces and hints deposited in
historical traditions. Though we are aware of a spectrum of
possible origins in the Bible, what we most dependably possess is the text framed by tradition as the object of our reading. Now, a sophisticated contemporary reader like Damrosch
would no doubt hasten to object that what he is proposing is
by no means the death of reading but rather a new model of
reading, one that encompasses opposing trajectories of meaning, simultaneously deconstructing and reconstructing the
biblical text. That is indeed a heroic undertaking, but it is
based in part on that trusting discrimination of divisions in
the text deriving from the hermeneutic circle Josipovici
describes—deriving, that is, from an analytic imposition on

the text of historical preconceptions that compromise the open responsiveness of reading.

The concluding note of Josipovici's observation points toward a central emphasis of his book on the substantive—as against the textual—peculiarity of the Bible as literature. The Bible is obviously not a book, or set of books, intended to be read for entertainment with an admixture of insight and information as, say, one might read a novel by David Lodge or John LeCarré. Rather, it wants to "draw me out of myself," using the medium of narrative to transform my sense of the world, urgently alert me to spiritual realities and moral imperatives I might have misconceived, or not conceived at all. Given this radical aim, and given the fact, as one recent analyst has argued,[4] that there is no explicit evidence of anything like our practice of reading for pleasure in the biblical world, not even a verb that corresponds to *reading* in our sense, how can the categories of literature be applied at all to the Bible?

First, it needs to be observed, as Josipovici himself aptly does, that in the Western tradition the notion of a literature that makes imperative claims on the reader quite transcending the "merely" literary is by no means restricted to the Bible. If we read novels like *Vanity Fair* and *Lost Illusions* for pleasure together with a certain amount of "instruction" about social institutions and moral behavior, there are other novels from the same era, like *Moby-Dick*, *War and Peace*, and *The Brothers Karamazov*, that use their narrative inventions as a means of imposing on the reader a troubling, potentially transformative vision of God, man, history, and nature. The paradox is that for readers to be challenged, disturbed, scared, spiritually prodded, emotionally battered by a book in no way precludes their taking pleasure in what the writer has wrought—the resonance and shapeliness of the language, the vividness of the realization of scene, the moral subtlety of represented motives and actions and relationships. The drowning of the boy Pip in *Moby-Dick* confronts us with something abysmal, but the haunting prose in which it is evoked mixes cognitive pain with readerly pleasure, and the same could be said for much of biblical narrative, from Jacob's desperate wrestling through the night with the angel to David's anguish over the death of his infant son.

The argument, then, that the Bible has almost no notion of literature as entertainment does not mark it off so drastically from later literatures as might first appear to be the case. And though there are many aspects of the Bible's literary vehicle that are peculiar to it, as we began to see in considering the oddness and unevenness of the text, it must also be stressed that writers in different ages and traditions, after all, have a finite spectrum of formal possibilities available to them, so there will necessarily be many continuities and striking analogies in literary expression from ancient to modern, from China to Peru. A gulf of historical and cultural differences separates the author of the Samson story from Gustave Flaubert, but both have to work with transitions and contrasts between narration and dialogue, with the structuring of narrative through correspondences of incident and scene, with recurring motifs, and with a choice between the representation and occultation of motive. In Flaubert's case, we know that there was a leisured audience that paid good money for his novels in order to enjoy them in the privacy of their homes, and there was certainly no counterpart to such a group in the biblical world. But however public the biblical audience, however pressing the historiographical and religious concerns of the writers, the articulation of the texts they fashioned offers abundant evidence for continuities between their activity and that of later, secular writers. There are certain things you do when you construct a story, whatever its purposes, as there are certain things you do when you design a building, whether you are an architect of sanctuaries or of pleasure palaces.

Here is a modest but thoroughly characteristic example. When David first flees from Saul (the very beginning of 1 Samuel 20), he comes to Jonathan, "and he said before Jonathan, 'What have I done? What is my crime and what is my transgression before your father that he should seek my life?'" As a link in a historical report, we need to know about this protestation of David's innocence in the face of Saul's hostility and about Jonathan's profession of unflagging friendship to David that will immediately follow. But this bit of dialogue is shaped with considerable artfulness, and it is surely not unreasonable to assume that the reader, or rather the ancient listener, was expected to admire or relish it, for art is after all made for an audience, not just for the effect. Let us note, then, that though Jonathan's affection for David has already been reported, as well as his direct discourse to David (at the beginning of the preceding chapter), this is the very first piece of dialogue addressed by David to Jonathan. What is remarkable, and quite characteristic of the representation of David in the first half of his career, is that it is more a speech than an intimate communication. In the narrator's language, David does not say his words *to* Jonathan, as he would in normal Hebrew idiom, but *before* (*lifney*) Jonathan, just as any actions he has or has not performed take place *before* the king. The implication of the odd preposition is public stance, public address. And, indeed, the words he uses exhibit the studied anaphoric pattern of a piece of oratory: "What have I done? What is my crime and what is my transgression . . . ?"

This cameo appearance of David as self-exculpating orator is beautifully consistent with a pattern I first described in *The Art of Biblical Narrative*[5]: throughout the story of the rise of David, his intimate feelings and motives are kept opaque, while every statement or seeming self-revelation he makes proves to be a public utterance, possibly calculated for political effect. David's friendship with Jonathan may well be his strongest personal bond, and Jonathan on his part has already shown his readiness to risk a great deal for the sake of David. Yet David's first reported speech to Jonathan is less a cri de coeur or personal revelation of friend to friend than a rhetorical performance contrived to make clear to the prince, and perhaps to anyone else who might be listening or to whom Jonathan might report the speech, that David is the guiltless victim of unjustified persecution. The author of the David story has, no doubt, purposes rather different from those of Jane Austen; but because both exploit some of the same formal resources of narrative, it is as true in the Book of Samuel as in *Pride and Prejudice* that the nice modulations of dialogue are subtle indices of characterization and of the definition of particular moments of speech in a complex network of relationships and events.

As long as the specimen is carefully chosen and sufficiently microscopic—the example we just considered comprises three words of reporting speech and eleven of reported speech in the Hebrew text—it is easy enough to show formal correspondences between biblical narrative and later fiction. But I hardly want to claim that a literary critic is confronted with precisely the same issues in Samuel and Genesis as in *Pride and Prejudice* and *The Red and the Black*. In order to highlight the differences, let me cite a more or less adjacent example from 1 Samuel in which both the textual bumpiness of biblical narrative and its concern with a realm not typically treated in later fiction are evident.

When Saul is first anointed by Samuel, he encounters a band of prophets and is infected with their ecstasy or frenzy. Precisely the same event recurs when he is losing his grip on the throne, just after he has driven David away. Since in both instances the episode concludes with a citation of the evi-

dently proverbial saying "Is Saul, too, among the prophets?"
it looks as though this narrative doubling—surely an improbability by the standards of later realism—is a consequence, as
I dutifully noted in *The Art of Biblical Narrative*,⁶ of an editorial
insertion of two competing etiological tales that explained the
origins of the saying. Although I also conceded at the time
that there might be some thematic purpose in the use of the
two versions, I would now shift the emphasis in the light of
my understanding of how biblical narrative utilizes disparate
materials.

The first occurrence of Saul's encounter with the prophets
immediately follows Samuel's prediction of the event to Saul.
It is in fact the climactic third in a folktale sequence of three
events that Samuel—who calls them "signs"—invokes. First
Saul will meet men who will tell him his father's asses have
been found; then he will meet three pilgrims headed for the
sanctuary at Bethel carrying three kids, three loaves of bread,
and a skin of wine. Then he will meet the band of prophets,
playing the musical instruments they use to induce a state of
trance. (The third sign is linked with the second not only by
the association with the sacred but also by a pun: *nevel*, "wine-
skin," also means "lyre," the first of the musical instruments
mentioned in 1 Samuel 10:5.) Here is the narrative report of
Saul's encounter with the band of ecstatics: "And they [Saul
and his servant] came there to the hill [or, Gibeah], and, look,
a band of prophets was headed toward him. And the spirit of
God seized him and he was transported ["prophesied"] in
their midst, and so when all who knew him before saw him
and, look, with the prophets he was in transport, people
would say to one another, 'What has happened to the son of
Kish? / Is Saul, too, among the prophets?' And one man there
spoke out and said, 'And who is their father?' [The text may
be corrupt here.] Thus it became a proverb: 'Is Saul, too,
among the prophets?'" (1 Sam. 10:10–12).

I have noted with a slash mark that the parallel questions of the people form the two halves of a line of parallelistic verse: in the Hebrew, there are three accented syllables in each statement, and as frequently happens with proper names in verse, as a substitute for the synonymous parallelism of common nouns, the person in question is referred to once by his patronymic and once by his proper name. I mention the switch into verse because here it is a formal sign of material that appears to have been introduced into the text from a folkloric source. This line of verse codifies the etiological question. The saying itself seems to refer to a surprising conjunction of disparate and contradictory terms, like sow's ears and silk purses or bulls and china shops. The tale of Saul going into a prophetic trance when he falls in with the band of ecstatics is an explanation of the perhaps enigmatic proverb. It should be observed that not all the details of Samuel's prediction appear in the narrative report of the event: no musical instruments are mentioned, and it is not clear that the prophets are coming down from a hilltop altar, as they are said to do in Samuel's predictive version. All this leads one to conclude that verses 10–12 are what biblical scholars call an "independent literary unit" that has been incorporated in the text.

There are still other seam lines in the text. Samuel concludes his prediction of Saul's ecstasy with the prophets (1 Sam. 10:6) by saying, "And you will turn into another man." The actual report of the event makes no mention of this crucial notion of metamorphosis that defines the experience with the ecstatics as a rite of passage into kingliness. Verse 9, in which "God gave him [literally, "turned," the same verb as in verse 6] another heart" *before* the encounter with the prophets, looks suspiciously like an editorial intervention, perhaps an attempt to compensate for the lack of reference to spiritual transformation in the language of the etiological tale proper.

A literary criticism accustomed to work with unitary

texts—say, the finished product of *Madame Bovary* that Flaubert refined out of more than three thousand pages of draft materials—ought not to proceed as though the biblical narrative were the same sort of seamless object. But the literary critic must also resist the notion that the biblical text is a more or less unwitting accretion of traditionary materials, or that the sundry materials can be identified historically and ideologically with sufficient certainty to allow him to describe them coherently as a diachronic "dialogue."

The text as we have it represents something like a collage. The writer—I would argue, even the original writer before the redactor—assumed that the act of literary composition involved, or at least could freely avail itself of, all sorts of texts—historiographical, etiological, genealogical, legal, legendary—circulating in the national tradition. The way the assembled textual collage works would suggest that the audience was conscious of its composite nature, accepted it as a matter of standard literary procedure. In our example, the writer wants to adopt for the initiation of the first king a formula from the dedication scene of the judges (that is, the ad hoc charismatic military leaders in the Book of Judges)—the act of being "seized" (the verb *tzalah*) by the spirit of God that figures equally in Samuel's prediction and in the narrator's report. For that purpose, the etiological tale about Saul among the prophets is nicely appropriate. But the writer also wants to modify the meaning of the formula from Judges. To begin with, it first occurs here in the third of the three predictions made by Samuel, seer and prophet, regarding the new king he has most grudgingly anointed, and, as Robert Polzin has suggested, it may be part of a strategy of assertion of control over Saul by the prophet: Saul is made to look like Samuel's puppet, undergoing everything Samuel says he will undergo, step by step.[7] The seizure by the divine spirit is only here represented as a kind of contagion from a group of professionals.

Only in this passage, moreover, do we get the idea, through the words the writer puts in the mouth of Samuel, that the descent of the spirit involves a change of identity, not merely an igniting of the self but its displacement by another self.

The writer's sense, then, of the spiritually daunting nature of kingship and of Saul's dubious qualification for it is vividly conveyed by his reshaping of the formula borrowed from Judges. The folktale about Saul among the prophets admirably suits this aim. One may infer that the general procedure for biblical writers using disparate sources was to respect the textual integrity of embedded material and not to trouble about any minor discrepancies with the surrounding story that might ensue. It is not important, for example, that the catalog of musical instruments of Samuel's prediction is absent from the etiological tale (and though they are unmentioned, one is free to imagine them). What is decisive is that the author, in establishing a careful context of his own for the tale, has given it a new meaning, his meaning.

The subject of this narrative, moreover, is an order of experience beyond the scope of most secular fiction. Although the Book of Samuel is one of the most shrewdly realistic political narratives in all of Western literature, behind the brilliantly represented play of personalities and power is a looming worldscape of uncanny forces and divine intentions transcending the realm of merely human politics. Saul is to be the first king of a people that has God's name inscribed in its own. Can any human being be truly fit for such a role? This dedication for kingship—as it proves, a failed dedication—is a shattering event that cancels the old self, flings the man into a spiritual maelstrom undreamed of in the Benjaminite farm of his boyhood. What this means, what it might have meant for the ancient audience, is not easy to imagine. A narrative in many respects compellingly realistic brings us to the limits of rational understanding.

The second occurrence of the tale of Saul among the prophets instructively confirms both the artful use of composite materials and the ultimate uncanniness of the subject of the narrative. David, in flight from Saul, has taken refuge with Samuel at the prophet's headquarters in Ramah. Here the band of prophets is represented virtually as a military contingent. Samuel on the promontory "stands over" the prophets, who appear to form a defensive line around him. Saul sends three waves of messengers, but each in turn is flung into ecstasy, bowled over by the manic power that inhabits the prophets. (A close parallel to this sequence of three waves sent from monarch to prophet appears in 2 Kings 1, where King Ahaziah sends in succession three contingents of soldiers with their captains to the prophet Elijah, who causes the first two to be consumed by divine fire and relents with the third.) Then Saul himself approaches the site, and this is what he gets for his trouble: "And the spirit of God came upon him, too, and he walked along in ecstasy [perhaps, "speaking ecstatically," "prophesying"] until he reached Naioth in Ramah. And he, too, stripped off his clothes and lay naked all that day and all that night. Thus do they say, 'Is Saul, too, among the prophets?'" (1 Sam. 19:23–24).

The duplication of the story in Chapter 10 and Chapter 19 obviously violates probability and linear logic. That is, if the proverb arose from a famous encounter between Saul and the prophets, the incident logically should have occurred either at the beginning of his reign or after his alienation from Samuel's protégé David, but not at both points in his career. How are we to conceive of this seeming contradiction? P. Kyle McCarter, Jr., in his scrupulous commentary on Samuel, duly notes that Saul "is now more a victim of prophetic inspiration than a beneficiary of it." But, with his eye on the evolution of the text, he resists the idea that this thematic antithesis might reflect artistic deliberateness:

> We are obliged by these facts [the facts cited include the con-
> tradictions between 10:10–12 and 19:18–24] to regard 19:18–24
> as a late addition to the narrative in the spirit of the prophetic
> revision of other materials but of independent origin, which
> was introduced in order to report another bit of tradition about
> David, Saul, and Samuel, which may have grown up as an
> explanation of . . . the saying . . . in circles where the alternative
> explanation was not known or accepted.[8]

This "obligation" by the facts has a ring of scientific precision, in the classic manner of biblical scholarship, but the
empirical basis on which the assertion rests is quite shaky.
Does the dramatic power exhibited by the prophets in the
story really reflect "prophetic revision" as a matter of the editorial history of the text? Perhaps the story in Chapter 19 does
have an "independent origin," but we know nothing of the
actual origins or of the "circles" in which the tale is said to
"have grown up," and there is no compelling reason for
excluding the possibility that the writer himself actually recast
the etiological tale he inserted in Chapter 10 in order to make
it serve his thematic purposes at this later juncture, in order to
use it as a studied antithesis. But what seems to me most misconceived in McCarter's account is his claim that this purported late addition (and do we know it is later than the other
tale?) "was introduced in order to report another bit of tradition." The assumption is characteristic of biblical scholarship
since the nineteenth century: the text is imagined to be driven
by a compulsion to report bits and pieces of tradition, with
scarcely any sense that the writer might be purposefully
selecting, embedding, reshaping, and recontextualizing bits
and pieces of tradition in his own artful narrative. What I
would argue for is a reading that takes into account the
bumpiness of the text without rushing to break the text down
into a series of bumps and disjunctions produced by the sheer
momentum of reporting tradition.

The Dutch scholar J. P. Fokkelman, a champion of redactorial or perhaps even authorial integralism, sees the discrepancy between the two tales of Saul among the prophets as a brilliantly pointed antithesis:

> The same faculty for the numinous and the same sensitivity for suddenly being lifted into a higher state of consciousness, which occurred there [in 10:10–12] under the positive sign of election, appear here under the negative sign of being rejected and now bring Saul into a lower state of consciousness, a kind of delirium. . . . One belongs with the other, the negative and the positive ecstasy are two sides of the same coin.[9]

Although Fokkelman, unswervingly focused on the discrimination of artful patterns, does not register the composite nature of the text in his critical account, as I think one ought to, he seems to me much closer to the dynamics of ancient Hebrew narrative than McCarter is. The ostensible discrepancies between the two versions of the etiological tale as well as the improbability of a second occurrence of the event fade in the revelatory light of what the writer has achieved thematically and psychologically by introducing two different treatments of the story at different junctures in his plot.

In the second version, there is no mention of Saul's turning into another man. Here Samuel stands quite properly as a kind of commander over the band of prophets because the point of the narrative is the opposition between presiding prophet, brandishing his power, and virtually deposed, powerless king. The rite of initiation and empowering has become a rite of rejection and leveling. The most striking new element in the story is that Saul strips and lies—or perhaps rather rolls—in ecstasy on the ground all that day and all that night. If the writer found this detail in an etiological tale that had general currency, it was a bit of serendipity; if instead he revised the previous etiological tale, it was a brilliant revision.

Time stops for the frantically pursuing king as he is prostrated
by prophecy, virtually paralyzed by it, all day and all night.
The nakedness reduces him to abject equality with all the
other victims of the spirit; and even more significantly, as a
recurring motif in 1 Samuel, nakedness signifies divestment of
kingship. When Samuel first rejected Saul, the pleading king
clung to the hem of the prophet's cloak, tearing it, upon which
Samuel declared, "The Lord has torn away from you the kingship of Israel this day" (1 Sam. 15:28). Later, at the cave near
Ein-Gedi, David will cut off a corner of the sleeping Saul's
cloak and then will be smitten with remorse over this symbolic action. Saul naked among the prophets—surely a new,
shocking twist to "Is Saul, too, among the prophets?"—is
physically realizing his terrible destiny, which will be grimly
completed when his body lies on the battlefield at Mount
Gilboa and the victorious Philistines "strip" (the same verb)
his armor after cutting off not the corner of a garment but his
head.

These observations point to the conclusion that biblical narrative—not just in its microtextual units but also in its larger
sequences—evinces an impressive degree of complex compositional artistry, even if the composition involved some cutting and pasting either by the writer or by the redactor or by
both. Thus, an order of critical attention honed on a reading of
Flaubert and Joyce is in certain respects appropriate to biblical
narrative, though of course there are manifest differences in
the way the ancient text was produced and in the textual contours of the narrative. Though it may sound odd, we are in
fact better readers of biblical narrative because we are lucky
enough to come after Flaubert and Joyce, Dante and
Shakespeare.

The remaining, powerful peculiarity of the Bible is that it is
a literature steeped in the quirkiness and imperfection of the
human that is ultimately oriented toward a horizon beyond

the human. In the example we have been considering, the presence of the inexplicable is even more spectacularly manifest in the second version of the tale than in the first. The story of Saul is one of the great portraits of a personality caught in the deadly mesh of politics. The gangling son of a prosperous farmer, moved by filial concern for his father (see 1 Sam. 9:5), perhaps not overly bright, he is at first haunted by doubt as to whether he is fit for the responsibilities of kingship: in the second of the three election stories that the writer deems necessary to represent his rise to the throne, he is "trapped" (*nilkad*) by lottery for the role, and the people find him hiding among the baggage (1 Sam. 10:20–21). Having become king, he suffers a compulsion to seize on signs and portents and to make rash vows, and at moments he is pathetically vulnerable to the fulminations and manipulations of Samuel, the man who anointed him king. Between his rejection by Samuel and the appearance of David, he enters into what looks like a manic-depressive cycle, and David's meteoric rise makes the young man a focus of the troubled king's paranoia. In all these respects, Saul is as persuasive a representation of man the political and psychological animal as any of the most memorable figures in Shakespeare's history plays. But there is something more that impinges on the life of Saul and ultimately determines it, something manifested in our story in the way the spirit—the Hebrew word also means "wind"—devastates him like a dark tornado.

The one thing modern readers should not do, even if they have secularist scruples, in regard to this dimension of biblical literature is condescend to it as "primitive." I also think that a merely psychologizing approach cannot do justice to the imaginative and spiritual seriousness of the ancient writer, though terms like *the unconscious, the irrational,* and *the uncanny* that tilt in the direction of the psychological would seem to be the best translation of such biblical moments into the idiom of our own culture. The Hebrew Bible is animated by an untiring, shrewdly perceptive fascination with the theater of human behavior in the textual foreground, seen against a background of forces that can be neither grasped nor controlled by humankind. (The New Testament tends to reverse the relation between background and foreground or, at any rate, to make the background obtrude more into the foreground.) The Bible has invited endless exegesis not only because of the drastic economy of its means of expression but also because it conceives of the world as a place full of things to understand in which the things of ultimate importance defy human understanding.

Gabriel Josipovici, in the conclusion of his book, beautifully observes this point. Noting how Thomas Mann, midrashically rewriting Genesis and Exodus in *Joseph and His Brothers*, is driven to *explain* everything in the narrative, Josipovici argues that this attachment to graspable truth runs counter to the underlying movement of the Bible. In his view, the most characteristic moments of biblical narrative "bring us face to face with characters who can be neither interpreted nor deconstructed. They are emblems of the limits of comprehension. What is important about them is precisely that they *are*, not that they *mean*."[10] Let me add that such a view of reality and how to represent it in narrative is by no means primitive and ought to appear all the less so after literary and philosophical modernism: the world is seen as offering all sorts of access to human understanding, but there is also no absolute fit between the nature of reality and the human mind. The biblical tale is fashioned in ways that repeatedly remind us of that ontological discrepancy.

There is little to be gained, I think, by conceiving of the biblical God, as Harold Bloom does, as a human character—petulant, headstrong, arbitrary, impulsive, or whatever. The repeated point of the biblical writers is that we cannot make sense of God in human terms. This perception is especially clear in passages like the two we have been considering in which God himself as a speaking agent does not appear but rather his spirit/wind. The divine spirit, like a high-voltage current, is a dangerous business: it can energize and transform, but it also can paralyze and destroy. In narrative terms, everything is a matter of shifting context. Saul at Naioth in Ramah perhaps still recalls the earlier moment when the spirit exalted him on his way to a kingdom; he certainly fails to understand how drastically the context has changed, the spirit having become a lethal weapon directed against him. On a larger scale, in the great narrative sequence from Genesis to Kings, divine election and the entering into a covenant with God are potentially ambiguous acts fraught with peril as well as with promise. The stories suggest that not only elation and pride but also anxiety and misgiving are appropriate responses to the idea of marrying personal or national destiny with a God whose inscrutable name is an alphabetic permutation of being itself.

I am proposing, in sum, that the Bible requires from the critic both the most fine-tuned attentiveness to its formal articulations and a kind of intellectual humility. It seems more than ever not an antiquarian book or a historical document but a literature that speaks to us urgently, with the power to "draw us out" of ourselves. It is able to do this in part because it scrutinizes the human condition with such a probing, unblinking gaze that is conveyed in the most subtle narrative vehicle, whatever its evolution and its composite character. But it is also able to do this by the boldness with which it represents human figures confronted, challenged, confounded by a reality beyond human ken. The literature of the Bible is still readable because in many of its conventions and formal

devices and strategies of organization it has a deep kinship
with other literature that we read. At the same time, the imaginative authority of the Bible is inseparable from its stubborn
peculiarity, and a modern literary criticism of the Bible needs
to respect that difference even as it revels in the fresh discovery of an ancient literary kin.

CHAPTER 2

Biblical Imperatives
and Literary Play

For many readers, it has been something of an embarrass-
ment that there should be literature in the Bible, or that the
Bible should ever be thought of as literature. If it is revealed
truth, if it is meant as a guide to the moral life and a source of
theological principle, if it is the authoritative account of the
first and last things, what, after all, does it have to do with literature? Let me hasten to say that one does not have to be a
Bible Belt fundamentalist to entertain such views. T. S. Eliot,
in the years after his conversion to Anglicanism, several times
publicly reproved those who read the Bible for its poetry
instead of for its religious truth. More recently, much the
same argument, couched in slightly different terms, has been
made by the eminent Bible scholar James Barr and by the dis-
tinguished critic and poet Donald Davie. Readers as subtle as
these hardly want to deny the presence of remarkable literary

qualities in the Bible, but they prefer to regard them as accidental by-products, or at best as felicitous embellishments, of the imperative religious concerns that are the heart of Scripture.

This way of seeing Scripture is continuous with the consensus of two millennia of Jewish and Christian interpretive tradition, and over the past two centuries it has been oddly reinforced by the dominant emphasis of academic biblical studies. The critical-historical investigation of Scripture, in the process of providing genuine illumination for much that was long obscure, has tacitly assumed a kind of Lockean distinction between primary and secondary qualities of the Bible. The former, deemed susceptible to scientific inquiry, include the philological constituents of the text, variously accessible through comparative Semitic studies; the sundry elements of historical context reflected in the text, often clarified by archaeological or other extrabiblical evidence; and the conjectured stages of evolving traditions that produced the text. The literary features of the text, on the other hand, have by and large been relegated to the status of secondary qualities, suitable mainly for discussion in the effusive appreciations of aesthetes and amateurs, but hardly worthy as objects of serious scholarship.

This marginalization of the Bible's literary characteristics presupposes a peculiarly limited notion of literature—a notion, one suspects, especially congenial to German professors of the preceding century who wrote sentimental verse at the age of eighteen and afterward scrupulously devoted themselves to the pursuit of graver matters. The idea of literature as a kind of elevated hobby for sensitive souls, an appurtenance to life's more urgent enterprises, leaves scant room not only for Dante, Dostoevski, and Blake but also for Shakespeare, Stendhal, Tolstoy, Joyce, and Faulkner. Gabriel Josipovici, in his recent study *The Book of God*, which is a kind of long and bold meditation on the status of the Bible as literature and its relation to later ideas of literature, aptly proposes that the Bible stands with a whole family of literary texts that seek—fiercely and in the end futilely—to transcend their own status as literature through necessarily literary means. Among writers of our own century, he mentions Proust, Kafka, Beckett, and Celan as figures who share with the creators of the Bible an aspiration to "produce something which is other than literature, something essentially truer and more necessary than literature could ever be."[1] This dream of self-transcendence, I would suggest, merely reproduces at the level of moral or spiritual expression a dynamic intrinsic to the evolution of all literature, however worldly or secular, which is constantly to reshape inherited conventions and genres in some fashion that will seem to go beyond their manifest artificiality. Thus, as Harry Levin has observed of the history of realism in the novel, writers from Cervantes to Flaubert to Joyce achieve an illusion of reality by incorporating in their fiction through allusion and parody the contrastive instances of earlier, more patently artificial fiction.[2]

It remains a question whether the Bible does something absolutely distinctive with literature or with the use of literary means to transcend literature. Meir Sternberg's work, and, on a more modest scale, my own as well, has sought to uncover a distinctive poetics of biblical narrative fashioned for the special ends of the Bible's new monotheistic understanding of history and human nature. Northrop Frye, in an imaginative refurbishing of Christian typology, has offered an account of Old Testament and New as a beautifully interlocked system of symmetrically arranged archetypes, but this proves to be only an extreme and exemplary instance of literature in general as Frye had long perceived it. In quite another direction, a recent study by David Damrosch boldly attempts to synthesize a literary perspective with a critical-historical one by analyzing biblical narrative as a distinctive form that works through the interaction of the various historical strata it comprises.[3] (Damrosch properly admonishes all of us new literary students of the Bible for neglecting the background of ancient Near Eastern genres and the peculiar historical circumstances in which biblical literature evolved by uneven stages, but, as I noted in chapter 1, he is stuck with the opposite quandary of basing an analysis on scholarship's conjectural identification of discrete strata in the texts and on the still shakier dating of the proposed strata.)

Perhaps the most powerful of all the recent attempts to render an account of the Bible's distinctive literary character is Harold Fisch's new book, *Poetry with a Purpose.*[4] I would like to reflect on Fisch's challenging argument because it illustrates so instructively the essential difficulty of talking about this subject. It is in some ways very helpful, in others misconceived, and the distance between the former and the latter is roughly marked by the way Fisch's position slides from one like that of Gabriel Josipovici to one like that of T. S. Eliot. Let me isolate what I think are the three essential points in Fisch's conception of biblical literature. I will list them in descending order of plausibility.

A great deal of biblical poetry, Fisch argues, is informed by what he suggestively describes as "a poetics of violence." The poetry of the Prophets or the poetry of the Song of Moses (for which he provides a splendid analysis) does not read like the tradition of verse derived from Greco-Roman origins. Fisch notes the prominence in poetic texts of the Hebrew verb *hpk*, "to overthrow," and proposes that "as against the rhythm of the natural world, we have a different rhythm, one that carries with it the ever-present potentiality of sudden divine interventions."[5] Commenting on Hosea and the other prophets, he develops, like Herbert Schneidau before him, the notion of a biblical swerve from myth to history and covenant,

away from "roundedness and closure" and toward "discontinuity and violence."[6]

Coupled with this notion of a poetics of violence is the
assumption that God in the inscrutability of his absolute purposes is implicit in all biblical texts, beyond beauty and artifice, ultimately negating any such secular or merely literary
values. At first glance, this seems an unexceptionable application of orthodox principle to literary analysis, but, as we shall
see in a moment, it becomes problematic when it is applied
even to texts like Esther and the Song of Songs that do not
mention God.

The most ingenious and the least persuasive of Fisch's
main theses is that biblical literature as a whole represents a
subversion of poetic genres in the interests of its monotheistic
"purpose." Thus, Deuteronomy 32, the Song of Moses, sub-
verts the pastoral; a passage in Lamentations "reads like a
veritable confrontation between pastoral and antipastoral"[7];
tragedy is deflected and subverted in Job, lyric in Psalms,
"pagan epic" in Esther, and carnal love poetry in the Song of
Songs. What we have here is essentially an application to the
Bible of Stanley Fish's notion of the "self-consuming artifact"
originally developed as an account of Protestant English literature of the seventeenth century, and I find it too Protestant
by half. The most salient difficulty is that Harold Fisch's
superimposition of the idea on the Bible is ahistorical. There
was no ancient Near Eastern Theocritus, and there is scant
evidence of a pastoral genre in this region during this era that
the poet of Deuteronomy 32 would have been aware of as
something to subvert. (The juxtaposing of two generic models
out of historical context may have its own validity, but Fisch
makes larger claims for his argument.) Again, one may question whether there was any real equivalent of a Greek lyric
genre in the ancient Near East, and Fisch is compelled to date
the Book of Job at least a century later than scholarly consen-

sus will allow in order to see in it a Hebrew response to
Aeschylus and thus a subversion of tragedy.

The supposed undoing of pagan genres in the Bible need
detain us no further, but the overarching idea with which it is
linked—that God's imperative presence in these poems and
stories is pervasive and absolute—must be seriously confronted. For if the commanding God of creation, covenant,
and history is everywhere, can there be any place for the play
of literary invention except in the insistent service of his purposes? The Book of Esther, where there is no actual reference
to God, is an instructive test case. Superficially, it looks like an
antithesis to that stark Hebrew narrative fraught with background that Erich Auerbach described so memorably in his
classic discussion of the Binding of Isaac. But Fisch proposes
intriguingly that Esther's ornate tale of imperial glitter is contrived to be undermined by a very different, urgent, God-
haunted story submerged within it:

> Thus, in the book of Esther is imbedded a Hebrew type of nar-
> rative, marked by a realism in which nothing is on the surface,
> everything standing out against the darkness of its own back-
> ground. Mordecai is the sign of this other narrative, Mordecai
> shrouded in darkness beyond the gate of the palace while the
> feasting goes on within, a feasting to which he is totally indif-
> ferent and from which he is totally cut off.[8]

This reading, inspired by Auerbach, is imaginative and
evocatively expressed, but is it convincing? At an early
moment of the plot, and in part as a necessity of the plot,
Mordecai does stand outside the palace gates, but it is strange
to say that he is cut off from the feasting, for the plot is contrived to bring him into the center of the world of feasting and
regal pomp and circumstance. In fact, the story of Esther is a
vehicle *for instituting* a feast, and Mordecai's grand gesture at

the end as newly appointed viceroy is to enjoin an annual obligation of feasting on his fellow Jews—"that they should make them days of feasting and joy, and of sending portions one to another, and gifts to the poor" (Esther 9:22). To evoke an abstemious Mordecai swathed in darkness is to play the role of a critical Malvolio objecting to cakes and ale in a story where cakes and ale are paramount. The Book of Esther illustrates how hard it is to sustain generalizations about a biblical narrative style or even about a biblical outlook, because this particular text vividly expresses a festive, perhaps even saturnalian, view of life. There is abundant comedy here of a sort that would scarcely be allowed by the usual preconceptions about biblical gravity, and if it seems an exception to the rule, it may well exemplify the rabbinic interpretive principle of "the exception that comes to teach us about the rule." Feasting in Esther is intimately associated with sexual comedy, and the inventive deployment of sexual comedy in the story is not readily reconciled with the sober purposes of covenantal faith.

The tale begins, one recalls, by offering an account of a royal feast with all its sumptuous trappings at which Queen Vashti is summoned to display her beauty before the wine-befuddled male guests. What is implicitly stressed at the beginning is the physical separation between harem and king, women and men. Whether or not the original idea was for Vashti to display herself naked, as some medieval commentators proposed, the obvious implication of Ahasuerus's summons is his pride of sexual possession. It is not altogether clear if that possession is more than titular, a matter of mere display. In any case, after Vashti's grand refusal, the royal counselor Memucan sounds the alarm that unless Vashti is turned away, male dominance of wives throughout the empire will be undermined by this act of insubordination. The prelude to the main plot, then, strikes a note of male anxiety that points forward to the climax in which the ever malleable Ahasuerus will be subtly guided by his new consort Esther to do exactly what she requires of him.

The sequel to the prelude is a delicate dance of teasing possibilities that invites a reconsideration of conventional assumptions about Scripture, for the Bible is surely not supposed to tease. The most beautiful virgins available are brought to the capital from the length and breadth of the kingdom, and after each spends six months dunking in oil of myrrh and another six months in assorted perfumes and unguents, she is led to the royal bed for a night of amorous trial. If one may address a practical question to a fairy-tale fantasy, trial of what? The young women are all equally fragrant and lubricated, and being virgins, none has any sexual expertise by which she might plausibly offer the king some unexpected pleasure. Ahasuerus himself, hardly an energetic or assertive man, seems an unlikely figure to be up to this strenuous regimen of nightly erotic exercises. Is it conceivable that the reason he is said to "love" Esther above all the other women and choose her as queen is that with her alone he is able to perform the act? (The subsequent narrative, after all, shows that Esther is not only beautiful and loyal but also patient and quietly reassuring.) I am not, of course, suggesting that the text ever explicitly mentions royal impotence, but the comic specter of the idea may well be raised. The notion comes closer to the surface in Chapters 4 and 5, in the revelation of a hitherto unreported ritual of separation between harem and throne: anyone who appears uninvited before the king, including even his supposedly beloved queen, will be forthwith put to death unless the king responds to the appearance by holding out his golden scepter. Whether or not this corresponds to any actual court practice in the Persian period, it surely confirms our double sense of Ahasuerus as a man with a shaky scepter. Fortunately for her, Esther survives the trial in which her life hangs in the balance just as she alone survived the nocturnal trial of selection. Her uninvited appearance before the king is followed by a party *à trois* on two successive days to which she invites him together with Haman. At the climactic moment of the second party, when she has announced that Haman intends to destroy her and all her people, the king walks out onto the terrace in a fit of wrath and consternation.

At this point, the teasing possibilities of sexual undermeaning that I have traced are made entirely explicit: Haman, in desperation, flings himself on the couch where Esther is reclining in order to plead for his life; the king, turning back into the room and seeing Haman "fallen on the couch," cries out in royal indignation, "Does he intend to ravish the queen before me in my own house?" and Haman pales in terror (Esther 7:8). It is quite likely that a common ancient Near Eastern political rite is being invoked here: to take sexual possession of the king's consort or concubines (as Absalom did when he usurped his father's throne) was to proclaim legal possession of his political power. If Ahasuerus's momentary misperception of Haman as would-be rapist exposes the plotting vizier as a potential usurper, it also jibes with the sundry intimations, from Chapter 1 onward, of the king's rather uncertain dominion over the female sex: at the moment of the villain's unmasking, in a piece of comic invention by no means necessary to the plot, Ahasuerus imagines Haman assaulting the lovely woman he himself has possessed only intermittently, and perhaps precariously.

Not all Hebrew narrative is a version of the Binding of Isaac, with its stark conjunction of fire, wood, knife, and impending sacrifice, its breathtaking violation of human conceptions in man's terrible exposure before God. To be sure, Esther is a late text that gives us Hebrew narrative in a holiday mood, and the holiday mood is rare in the Bible. The

mere fact of its presence, however, is instructive. Although it
is evident that the biblical writers did not generally conceive
themselves as entertainers and that they were intent on conveying through narrative and poetry God's plan in creation
and in the history of Israel, the literary art they exercised so
splendidly was not always, or not entirely, subservient to religious ends. I realize that what I am saying may sound blas-
phemous, or at least excessively modernizing, to some, and so
I want to put in due perspective the claim I will proceed to
spell out.

The Hebrew writers do, of course, keep in steady focus
God and Israel, creation, covenant, and commandments
(though not very noticeably in Esther), and from moment to
moment all the subtleties of their literary art are exploited to
make palpable their God-driven vision of reality, together
with the individual and collective obligations dictated by it.
This is virtually a truism, and I think it requires the following
modest but important qualification: no writer, not even the
most intently religious one, can ever quite escape the momentum of the medium in which he works. The making of literature everywhere involves a free play of the imagination with
language, inventively using such elements as rhythm, repetition, musicality, imagery, character, scene, act, and symbol,
even when the writer's aim is to produce "something essentially truer and more necessary than literature." If virtually
every utterance of biblical narrative points toward the imperative concerns of covenantal faith, it is also demonstrably evident that virtually every utterance of biblical narrative reveals
the presence of writers who relished the words and the materials of storytelling with which they worked, who delighted,
because after all they were writers, in pleasing cadences and
surprising deflections of syntax, in complex echoing effects
among words, in the kind of speech they could fashion for the
characters, and in the way in which the self-same words could

be ingeniously transformed as they were passed from narrator to character, or from one character to another.

Let us consider the presence of this sense of writerly delight in two passages from texts more historically urgent than Esther, belonging to the classic age of Hebrew narrative that produced the chain of masterworks from Genesis to Kings. Now, a prominent and, I think, distinctive convention of this body of classic Hebrew narrative, which has been analyzed by Meir Sternberg, by George Savran, and by me, is the modification of dialogue in near-verbatim repetition in order to indicate the attitudinal angle, the changed audience, or even the downright mendacity of the speaker who repeats someone else's already cited words.[9] Understandably, in most of the examples of the technique that have been discussed—and the technique is used pervasively in this corpus of narratives—the moral or psychological or thematic definition of character is sharpened or somehow subtly advanced by the changes the character introduces into someone else's words. Thus, in 1 Kings 21, the false witnesses report to Jezebel that Naboth has been stoned to death, their words echoing the narrator's statement of that fact, but when she passes on this news to Ahab, she quietly deletes the unpleasant detail of stoning and prefaces the report of Naboth's death by telling Ahab he can now go ahead and take possession of the coveted vineyard.

Not all occurrences, however, of such "editing" by one character of another's speech are so evidently instrumental. A piquant case in point is the triangular relation of the narrator, Sarah, and the angel in Genesis 18 at the annunciation of the birth of Isaac. In this instance, as we shall see in a moment, the repeated bit of direct discourse is something thought, not audible speech:

And Abraham and Sarah were old, advanced in years, Sarah no longer had her woman's flow. And Sarah laughed

inwardly, saying, "After being shriveled, shall I have pleasure,
my husband being old?" And the Lord said to Abraham, "Why
is it that Sarah laughed, saying, 'Shall I really give birth, I being
old?'" (Gen. 18:11–13)

We have in rapid sequence three statements about the
advanced age of the future parents of Isaac—the narrator's,
Sarah's, and the angel's version of Sarah's statement (he is
referred to simply as the Lord, YHWH, in keeping with a frequent usage in Genesis, and perhaps may be construed as the
Lord rather than a messenger). The narrator's authoritative
report is balanced, emphatic, and in a sense neutral. There are
three brief clauses: the first flatly tells us that both Abraham
and Sarah are old; the second underscores the initial information by reiterating it synonymously; the third spells out
Sarah's condition of menopause, thus capping the couple's
great age before procreation with the one biological fact that
should make procreation an impossibility. The next sentence
is devoted to Sarah's review of this same narrative datum in a
brief interior monologue. It is introduced by the term "saying," *le'mor*, which is regularly used to introduce direct discourse, whether spoken or unspoken, throughout the Bible.
What is peculiar, and thematically weighted as we move
toward the birth of Isaac, "he who laughs," is that *le'mor* is not
preceded, as convention dictates, by a verb of speech, but by
"laughed," adverbially qualified by *beqirbah*, "inwardly."
Sarah, like the narrator, reflects that both she and her husband
are old, but she crucially modifies the human meaning of this
information through the new terms she chooses for it and the
new syntactic order in which she conveys it. She begins with
her own condition, which is now manifestly a plight, the subject of a complaint. She is not simply old but "shriveled" (the
Hebrew root *blh* means "worn-out" or "in rags" when applied
to garments, evidently the primary meaning of the term, and
"wasted" or "shriveled" when applied to flesh), and she can-

not imagine that she will again experience pleasure.

Though the immediate context, the promise of the birth of a son overheard by Sarah, could mean that the pleasure in question is the pleasure of maternity, the root of the word she uses, `ednah` (cognate with Eden), has connotations of sensual delight, and so it is likely that Sarah is referring to sexual pleasure or perhaps even, in a double-edged usage, to sexual pleasure leading to the joy of motherhood. (The conclusion of some philologists that `ednah` means "abundant moisture" would make the word point even more directly to sexual physiology.) The fact of menopause, though obviously implied, is not actually mentioned but instead displaced into Sarah's brooding over her withered body and her removal from conjugal gratification. Her husband's old age is invoked in a tacked-on clause at the end, the syntax yielding a progression of thought along the following lines: I am hopelessly ancient, and my husband is old, too. The three phrasal components of Sarah's interior monologue create a certain ambiguity of causal attribution quite typical of biblical characterization. Is Sarah beyond hope of pleasure because she is shriveled, as we initially suppose, or because she is stuck with an aged husband? The biblical writer's ability to produce complexities through the starkest economy of means is breathtaking. The objective data given in the narrator's report of a post-menopausal matriarch and an elderly patriarch are converted in her interior monologue into a woman's emotionally fraught statement of her biological predicament that might at the same time carry a hint of sexual resentment toward her aged husband.

When the Lord, or his emissary, reports Sarah's inward "laughing" to Abraham, a whole new set of transformations is introduced. Exercising as divine being the auditory equivalent of clairvoyance, he has obviously heard the unspoken words of disbelief of Sarah's interior speech, but what he chooses to report to Abraham is another matter. The most prominent change was noted long ago by the great medieval exegete Rashi—the deletion of any reference to Abraham's old age. Rashi phrases this touchingly: "Scripture made a change in the interests of domestic harmony [*mipney hashalom*], for she had said, 'My husband is old.'" Always a keen reader, Rashi is acute in observing the difference in the repetition, but it is noteworthy that he motivates it on implicitly didactic grounds: Scripture is eager to teach us through this example of divine speech that for the sake of domestic tranquillity it is important to exercise diplomacy. But the angel's version of Sarah's words is impelled by something other than didacticism, as may become clearer from the other alterations he makes. The angel not only omits the reference to Abraham's old age shared by Sarah and the narrator but also edits out all mention of female biology associated with Sarah's old age: his words to Abraham say nothing of the absent menses in the narrator's report or the shriveling and the deprivation of pleasure in Sarah's interior monologue; in his version, she expresses incredulity only over the simple fact that she could give birth.

The interesting question is why this whole set of changes should have been introduced. The narrative has come to a moment of high solemnity, when the seemingly impossible covenantal promise of progeny and future national greatness is repeated one last, climactic time. It is far from clear how the intricate triangular game of variation in repetition that we have been following contributes to this grand historical theme, or how it illuminates any of the spiritual imperatives that are the very purpose of Scripture. Why did the writer not simply transpose the narrator's words into the first person without further change for Sarah's interior monologue, and then allow the angel to quote her words verbatim in addressing Abraham? One can hardly say that he simply wanted to avoid the tedium of exact repetition, because the Bible abounds in examples of exact repetition, or at least in much closer approximations of it than we have here. In my view, the only plausible explanation is that the writer, for all the seriousness of his purpose to render the history of Israel as the history of the beginnings of redemption, was imagining Sarah, Abraham, and the angel or the Lord (despite himself?—we shall never know) as *characters.* Among my own past sins, I have managed to vex a number of critics by applying the term *fiction* to biblical narrative, though I did try to make clear that at least in my usage there was no contradiction between fiction and the intent effort of historical truth telling.

The angel eavesdropping on the interior speech of the eavesdropping Sarah on the other side of the tent flap is a nice microscopic illustration of the operation of the fictional impulse in Scripture. The writer is not content merely to report the essential data of covenantal history with the strictest efficiency or the optimal thematic emphasis. What he has done here is to imagine himself first into Sarah and then into the angel addressing her aged husband. The extraordinary economy of means employed in no way precludes a richness of imaginative identification. In just seven Hebrew words of interior monologue, Sarah is revealed not simply as an emblematic matriarch in a divine scheme but as a woman struggling under the load of a particular life experience, hyperconscious of her own withered flesh, resentful of her estrangement from the pleasures of the body, whether in maternity or sexuality or both, and perhaps resentful as well of her aged husband. The Divinity who overhears all of this deems it unsuitable for the ears of Abraham, who may have his own vulnerability as a man in his declining years never able to beget a child with the wife of his youth; who presumably has long since given up trying; and who ought not to be confronted with the biological details of his wife's geriatric condition—especially since the divine plan now requires him to feel the urge to cohabit with her.

Literary style, I have argued elsewhere, is an exercise of the expressive resources of language that seeks a nuanced precision beyond the reach of ordinary usage and at the same time exhibits a repeated delight in the sheer shaping of its materials, which is in fine excess of the occasion of communication.[10] Because this sense of writerly pleasure, in which the alert reader is invited to join, is manifest even in the darkest and most urgent of literary works, from *King Lear* to *The Brothers Karamazov* and *The Trial*, I have described it, perhaps a little provocatively, as "the high fun of the act of literary communication." There is evidence of its presence in almost every line of biblical narrative, and though the biblical writers are, of course, concerned with conveying "messages"—creedal, moral, historical, ideological—the lively inventiveness with which they constantly deploy the resources of their narrative medium repeatedly exceeds the needs of the message, though it often also deepens and complicates the message. The excess of which I speak is not at all like the supposed "supplement" in deconstructionist parlance that is produced by an endless sense of lack in the act of communication. On the contrary, it emerges from the writer's vivid intuition of a superabundance of possibilities suggested by the creative associations of his literary medium.

We began with a highly exceptional festive narrative where the free play of literary invention should hardly surprise us, and now we have encountered it operating on a more restricted scale, but nevertheless strikingly, in the patriarchal history of national origins. My concluding example, as a kind of limit case for my thesis, is a text in which the manipulation of style seems very much subordinate to thematic ends. Even in such an instance, however, the handling of narratorial report and dialogue pushes beyond the boundaries of thematic utility, hints at that collusive game between writer and audience that is the hallmark of literary narrative. I shall quote the very beginning of the story of Deborah (Judg. 4:4–5) in a flagrantly literal translation because the Hebrew here has a certain purposeful awkwardness that is smoothed over in all the conventional English versions: "And Deborah, a prophetwoman ['ishah nevi'ah], Lapidoth's woman, she was judging Israel at that time. And she would sit under the palm tree of Deborah. . . ." What is odd about these initial expository clauses in the Deborah story is the obtrusion of feminine gender and of the term *woman*. Since all Hebrew nouns are either masculine or feminine, the moment you hear *nevi'ah* and not *navi'* you realize that you are dealing with a prophetess, not a prophet. The superfluous *woman* in apposition with *prophetess* is immediately picked up in "Lapidoth's woman" (like the French *femme,* the same term means "wife" or "woman"). This foregrounding of the feminine is then reinforced by the introduction of an easily dispensable pronoun: "Deborah, . . . *she* was judging Israel." The use of the participial form at the beginning of the next verse (my translation renders it as an iterative verb) is the occasion for immediately repeating the feminine pronoun: "And *she* would sit" (*wehi' yoshevet*—an imperfect verb, *wateshev*, would have required no pronoun).

Let me suggest that the stylistic bumpiness at the beginning of the story is intended precisely to bump our sensibility as an audience. It is the rare exception and not the rule to have a prophetess rather than a prophet, a female rather than a male judge. A reversal of roles between woman and man, *'ishah* and *'ish*, will be at the heart of the story, with Deborah's role as commander perfectly complemented by Jael's role at the end as assassin of the enemy general: the reiteration of the thematic term in the Song of Deborah is noteworthy—"May

Jael be blessed above women, / woman of Heber the Kenite, / above women in tents may she be blessed" (Judg. 5:24). The first episode of the story is then a dialogue between a very hesitant male field commander, Barak, and the firmly insistent Deborah. Her initial words to him seem to assume a prior communication to which he has been unwilling to respond: "Has not the Lord commanded you. . . ." And the very first word of the Lord's message to Barak, which she quotes, is the masculine imperative verb *lekh*, "go." What happens to that verb in the immediately subsequent exchange between Barak and Deborah is almost comic. He says, "If you will go with me, I will go, and if you won't go with me, I won't go," and she answers, "Go, I will go [*halokh 'elekh*] with you, but it will not be your glory on the way you are going, for by the hand of a woman will the Lord deliver Sisera" (Judg. 4:8–9).

Literary students of the Bible have drawn abundant attention to what Buber and Rosenzweig first described as *Leitwörter*, "leading words," or thematic key words, by which the meanings of the narrative are progressively complicated through repetition. In this instance, the technique is pushed so far that it verges on self-parody. Barak, in a paroxysm of hesitation, releases a stammering chain of *go*'s, his going repeatedly conditional on Deborah's going, on her leading him by the hand along the way. This last idiom, which is not stated though perhaps implied, surfaces in another sense, with proleptic irony, in her reply to him. When she says that the Lord will deliver the Canaanite commander "by the hand of a woman," she is using what amounts to a lexicalized metaphor, with the sense of "by the power of" or "through the agency of," and which is a recurrent idiom in the frame-narratives of Judges (the Lord delivers X in or by the hands of Y). The subsequent narrative and poem then shockingly literalize the metaphor as Jael is seen with right hand on the hammer, left hand on the tent peg that she drives into Sisera's temples.

I do not mean to suggest that the author of the Deborah story is making some sort of programmatic feminist statement about the reversal of sex roles. On the contrary, whatever musings about such reversal the story may raise (and it is not alone in the Book of Judges in its concern with ambiguous gender relations) belong precisely to the realm of teasing possibility that is separable from the explicit ideological messages of the narrative, which involve a plea for national solidarity, a responsiveness to divine imperatives, and—beyond the frame of this story—a polemic against idolatrous backsliding. The piquant idea of the woman of manly courage and the pusillanimous man (Barak at the beginning) or the man of childlike helplessness (Sisera in Jael's tent) was appropriate for the writer to explore without explicit thematic assertion in the dialogue's play of *Leitwörter* and in the narrator's small deformations of idiom and syntax. Did he do this because he wanted to introduce a note of satiric rebuke to an Israelite nation unwilling to exercise requisite martial virtue (an idea that might have had some practical urgency for the original writer, if not for his later Deuteronomistic editor), or simply because he discovered an intrinsic allure in this surprising turnaround of sex roles?

What makes this narrative, like all literary narratives, interesting is that there is no simple accounting either for the writer's motives or for the range of implications to which his work points. The flickering presence of a perhaps gratuitous theme producing a hint of comic byplay in the midst of a presumably historical report of military triumph over Israel's enemies and the Lord's is an instance of that fine excess of the ostensible occasion of communication toward which the literary imagination constantly moves. Language, straining against the decorum of ordinary usage, is fashioned to intimate perspectives the writer would rather not spell out and invites our complicitous delight in the ingenuity of the fashioning.

The distinction I have tried to indicate is by no means one between form and content or between message and embellishment. Everything in the story contributes to an encompassing vision of history, social institution, human nature, individual character, and, of course, God. Part of this vision is a core of consciously held intentions to provide information and moral instruction—intentions that either address a national consensus or, perhaps more often, seek to create one. The wavering nature of the consensus is reflected in the fact that it contains at least some different items, sometimes conflicting ones, for different writers and in different periods. But one measure of the greatness of biblical literature is that the energy of its literary imagination led to a probing—at once playful and serious—of the borders of consensus and what lay beyond it even as the consensus was being forged through narrative.

It will be noted that all three of my examples involve the power or plight of women in what is generally presumed, with good warrant, to be a set of narratives dominated by men. These instances seem to me especially instructive because they show the literary imagination—perhaps inadvertently—testing the limits of biblical ideology. Such imaginative exploration of what lies beyond received values is characteristic of the dynamic of literary expression everywhere. Ideology tends to draw lines, insist on norms, in the interests of a particular system of governance and social relations. Literary invention, to a large extent because it involves the kind of free play of the imagination with a verbal and fictional medium that we have been following, often has the effect of calling ideological assumptions into question, or qualifying them ironically, or at any rate raising certain teasing possibilities counter to the accepted ideology. It may well be that the relation between the sexes, which is at issue in all the examples I have chosen, is a realm of experience that in most cultures offers an especially potent invitation for the literary artist to conjure with notions that run counter to established views. Two of the three texts we have considered involve not just gender roles but sexuality, a sphere that every culture tries to police in various ways but that stubbornly persists in the privacy of its enactment as a zone of freedom, a perennial outlet of free play for the body and perhaps for the spirit as well.

The literary imagination qualifies or challenges prevalent ideological assumptions not necessarily—in fact, not usually—because it has an ideological program of its own but, on the contrary, because its inventive, associative, and even formal engagement with its own verbal, narrative, and referential materials leads it to peer over the other side, or at the underside, of things as they are ordinarily seen. "The artist," as Leo Lowenthal has aptly put it, "is no Cartesian but rather a dialectician focusing on the idiosyncratic, on that which does not fit into the system. In short, he is concerned with human costs and thus becomes an ally of . . . the critical perspective."[11] Hence these remarkable moments in the notoriously patriarchal Bible when a woman's predicament or her ability to act forcefully is brought to the fore.

This tension between ideology and the literary imagination is not at all a split between content and form or between the moral and the aesthetic. On the contrary, the complex formal articulation of biblical literature is manifestly the means through which its moral, religious, and historiographical meanings are realized. As with literature elsewhere, meaning is here deepened and in a sense is discovered, through the exploration of form. Because the working of literary form is a kind of work that involves a dimension of free play, biblical literature, like its counterparts elsewhere, repeatedly offers us insights and pleasures that exceed the strict limits of ideological intention. In other words, the literary medium stretches ideology beyond any merely programmatic or doctrinal frame. An aged Sarah embittered by the burden of female biology, imagining herself mocked by portents, conveys to us a complex sense of the human costs of life under the sign of the covenant.

All this does not mean that the Bible is just like any other body of literature. On the contrary, its distinctive traits are so striking that one hardly needs to argue for their presence. The ancient writers, as Fisch, Josipovici, and countless others before them have observed, steadily sought to realize through the medium of literature an order of truth that utterly transcends literature. The anonymity and the collective viewpoint of biblical writing are tokens of this aspiration—no place is allowed for the self-promoting identity of the individual writer or for the ephemerality of merely private experience. The implicit drive, moreover, of the sundry biblical texts toward forming an overarching unity of statement about God, history, and creation also sets Scripture apart: Genesis, Judges, and Kings are not just literary works by different hands related through genre, like the novels of Dickens and Trollope, but complementary voices, harmonized by later editors, in an authoritative chorus of collective destiny. Even the dimension of imaginative free play that I have described is at least partly realized in distinctive ways because the drastic economy of biblical narrative usually means that the elements of fine excess are manifested at a more microscopic level of the text than is common in other literary traditions. Such manifestations are nevertheless abundantly evident throughout biblical narrative and are often as brilliantly inventive, sometimes even as playful, as anything to be encountered in secular literature. For the covenantal urgency of the biblical authors impelled them on a bold and finally impossible project: they sought to use literature to go irrevocably beyond itself, but, being writers of genius enamored, as writers always are, with how they could tap the endless resources of their medium, they could not avoid producing in their work an enchanting affirmation of the free-playing logic of literary expression.

CHAPTER 3

The Literary Character of the Bible

The difficulty of getting a bearing on the Hebrew Bible as a collection of literary works is reflected in the fact that we have no comfortable term with which to designate these books. Common usage in Western culture, following Christian tradition, calls them the Old Testament, a name originating in the assumption that the Old requires completion in the New or is actually superseded by the New. (The term itself, more properly rendered "new covenant," derives from the reading given in Hebrews 8:6–13 of a prophecy in Jeremiah 31:31, where the phrase first occurs. In Jeremiah it actually signals a grand renewal of Israelite national existence under God, but Hebrews takes it to mean the replacement of an "aging" covenant about to expire by a new one.) That is in fact how major writers from Augustine to Dante to Donne to Eliot have conceived Hebrew Scripture and absorbed it into their own work, and this conception is persistent enough to have figured centrally as recently as 1982 in a book by one of our most important critics, Northrop Frye's *The Great Code: The Bible and Literature*. The Jews collectively have rejected the term for all that it implies, and as a matter of literary history there is surely no warrant to imagine that the ancient Hebrew writers composed their stories and poems and laws and genealogical lists with the idea that they were providing a prelude to another set of texts, to be written in another language centuries later. Harold Bloom, a critic who has tirelessly studied the ways in which later writers appropriate the achievements of their predecessors for their own purposes, makes this point with witty incisiveness when he speaks of "the Christian triumph over the Hebrew Bible, a triumph which produced that captive work, the Old Testament."[1]

It is nevertheless a question what to call these books and how to think of them outside a state of captivity. The very term *Bible* (from the Greek *ta biblia*, "the books") is more a vague classification than a title. *Jewish Bible* refers to the choice and order of the texts made by rabbinic Judaism for its canon, and so in its own way it also represents an appropriation of the ancient writings by latecomers, though not so egregious a one as the Christian. *Hebrew Bible*, the term that Bloom prefers and that I shall use in what follows, comes closer to the originating literary facts, though it is not strictly accurate, for three post-Exilic books, Ezra, Nehemiah, and Daniel, are partly composed in Aramaic, a Semitic tongue merely cognate with Hebrew. Postbiblical Hebrew tradition itself has never enshrined a single title but instead has wavered among several that in different ways suggest the elusive heterogeneity of the corpus. Rabbinic literature refers to the Writings and to the Twenty-four Books. Most commonly, the Hebrew Bible has been designated by Jews as *Tanakh*, an acronym for *Torah* (Pentateuch), *Neviim* (Former and Latter Prophets), and

Ketuvim (miscellaneous Writings, or Everything Else), which is no more than a crude generic division of the books in their traditional order according to the Jewish canon. Finally, these books are often called *Miqra'*, especially in modern secular contexts, and that term simply indicates "that which is read," more or less in the sense of "the Text," and so will scarcely serve as a defining title.

Any literary account of the Hebrew Bible must recognize just this quality of extreme heterogeneity. From one point of view, it is not even a unified collection but rather a loose anthology that reflects as much as nine centuries of Hebrew literary activity, from the Song of Deborah and other, briefer archaic poems embedded in the prose narratives to the Book of Daniel (second century B.C.E.). The generic variety of this anthology is altogether remarkable, encompassing as it does historiography, fictional narratives, and much that is a mixture of the two, lists of laws, prophecy in both poetry and prose, aphoristic and reflective works, cultic and devotional poems, laments and victory hymns, love poems, genealogical tables, etiological tales, and much more.

One might imagine that religious ideology would provide the principle of selection for the anthology. In some minimal sense, that must be true. For example, no truly syncretistic or pagan texts are included, though it is perfectly plausible that there might have been ancient Hebrew compositions written in such a spirit. The Hebrew Bible itself occasionally refers to annalistic or possibly mythological works such as the Book of the Battles of YHWH and the Book of Yashar, which have not survived. (The oldest extant scrolls, it should be noted, are those found in the caves at Qumran, going back to the first century B.C.E.; as far as we know, whatever else was written in the ancient period in Hebrew on parchment or papyrus has long since turned to dust, so we can only guess at the full scope of this literature.)

But even within the limits of monotheistic ideology, there is a great deal of diversity in regard to political attitudes; conceptions of history, ethics, psychology, causation; views of the roles of law and cult, of priesthood and laity, of Israel and the nations, even of God. Indeed, when one contemplates the radical challenge in Job not only to the doctrine of retribution but to the very notion of a man-centered creation, or Ecclesiastes' insistence on cycles of futility in place of the linear, progressive time familiar from Genesis, or the exuberant eroticism of the Song of Songs, one begins to suspect that the selection was at least sometimes impelled by a desire to preserve the best of ancient Hebrew literature rather than to gather the consistent normative statements of a monotheistic party line. In fact, the texts that have been passed down to us exhibit not only extraordinary diversity but also a substantial amount of debate with one another.

But the idea of the Hebrew Bible as a sprawling, unruly anthology is no more than a partial truth, for the retrospective act of canonization has created a unity among the disparate texts that we as later readers can scarcely ignore; and this unity in turn reflects, though with a pronounced element of exaggeration, an intrinsic feature of the original texts—their powerfully allusive character. (For a more elaborate consideration of allusion in the Bible, see chapter 7.) All literature, to be sure, is necessarily allusive: writers are compelled in one way or another to make their text out of antecedent texts (oral or written) because it would not occur to them in the first place to do anything so unnatural as to compose a hymn or a love poem or a story unless they had some model to emulate. In the Hebrew Bible, however, what is repeatedly evident is the abundance of authoritative national traditions, fixed in particular verbal formulations, to which later writers respond through incorporation, elaboration, debate, or parody.

Perhaps, as a good many scholars have conjectured, these

formulations first circulated in oral tradition in the early, pre-monarchical phase of Israelite history. In any event, literacy is very old in the ancient Near East and there is no preliterate stage of full-fledged Israelite national existence; so there is no reason to assume that the activity of putting things down on a scroll (*sefer*; see, for example, Exod. 17:14) was not part of the formative experience of ancient Israel. The internally allusive character of the Hebrew texts—not to speak of allusions in them to non-Hebrew ancient Near Eastern texts—is more like the pervasive allusiveness of Eliot's *The Waste Land* or Joyce's *Ulysses* than, say, the occasional allusiveness of Wordsworth's *The Prelude*. In this central regard, the Hebrew Bible, because it so frequently articulates its meanings by recasting texts within its own corpus, is already moving toward being an integrated work, for all its anthological diversity.

Let me offer one relatively simple example. When Boaz first meets Ruth in the field, after she prostrates herself before him in response to his offer of hospitality and protection, he praises her in the following words: "It has indeed been told me, all that you have done for your mother-in-law since the death of your husband: how you left your father and your mother, and the land of your birthplace, and came unto a people you did not know before" (Ruth 2:11). There is a strong echo here, as surely anyone in the ancient audience would have recognized, of God's first, imperative words to Abraham that inaugurate the patriarchal tales: "Get you out of your land, and your birthplace, and your father's house, unto a land that I will show you" (Gen. 12:1). The identical verbal-thematic cluster, land-birthplace-father, stands out in both texts, though the author of Ruth adds "mother" to the configuration, understandably enough because his protagonist is a woman and because she takes Naomi, her mother-in-law, as a kind of adoptive mother when she abandons her homeland of Moab.

What is the point of the allusion? It sets Ruth up as a founding mother, in symmetrical correspondence to Abraham the founding father. She, too, comes from a foreign country to the east to settle in the Promised Land. God's next words to Abraham—"And I will make you a great nation, and I will bless you, and make your name great" (Gen. 12:2)—will also apply directly to her as the woman from whom David will be descended. Progenitrix as Abraham is progenitor, she, too, will have to overcome a palpable threat to the continuation of the family line for the fulfillment of the promise. The very encounter here of a future bride and groom in a pastoral setting involving the drawing of water (Ruth 2:9) recalls a series of similar patriarchal tales. And perhaps most pointedly in regard to the complex themes of the Book of Ruth, God's very first word to Abraham, *lekh*, "get you" (root *halak*), or simply "go," is made a chief thematic key word strategically reiterated in her story: again and again, we are reminded that her "going" from Moab is, paradoxically, a "returning" to a land she has never before seen, a return because it is now by choice her land. Thus, taking up the destiny of the covenanted people, for Ruth as for Abraham, means renouncing the filiations of geography and biology, replacing the old natural bonds with new contractual ones, as Abraham does with God, having left his father's house, and as Ruth does with the clan of Elimelech and the land of Judea.

The patriarchal text, trumpeting the departure from father and birthplace, announces a new relation to God and history; the text in Ruth, with a less theological and ultimately more political frame of reference, adopts the language of the earlier writer to define its own allied but somewhat different meanings: the tale of the foreign woman who becomes staunchest of kin through her acts of love and loyalty. Such intertextual play occurs repeatedly in the Hebrew Bible, drawing its disparate elements into a certain mobile, unpredictable unity.

My very invocation of the technique of allusion, some may object, presupposes what is most in need of demonstration—that the primary element that pulls the disparate texts together is literary. According to one common line of thought, the Hebrew Bible exhibits certain literary embellishments and literary interludes, but those who would present "the Bible as literature" must turn it around to an odd angle from its own original emphases, which are theological, legislative, historiographic, and moral. This opposition between literature and the really serious things collapses the moment we realize that it is the exception in any culture for literary invention to be a purely aesthetic activity. Writers put together words in a certain pleasing order partly because the order pleases but also, very often, because the order helps them refine meanings, make meanings more memorable and more satisfyingly complex, so that what is well wrought in language can more powerfully engage the world of events, values, human and divine ends. One hardly wants to deny the overriding spiritual earnestness of the ancient Hebrew writers; certainly what has survived of their work in the canon offers no more than occasional fleeting glimpses of the kind of playfulness often detectable in ancient Greek and Latin literature. And yet, a close study of these writings in the original discovers again and again, on every level from word choice and sentence structure to the deployment of large units of composition, a delight in the manifold exercise of literary craftmanship. (We have already seen some instances of this delight in chapter 2.) These writers are obviously intent on telling us about the origins of the world, the history of Israel, God's ethical requirements of mankind, the cultic stipulations of the new monotheistic faith, the future vistas of disaster and redemption. But the telling has a shapeliness whose subtleties we are only beginning to understand, and it was undertaken by writers with the most brilliant gifts for intimating character, defining scenes, fashioning dialogue, elaborating motifs, and balancing near and distant episodes, just as the God-intoxicated poems of the psalmists and prophets evince a dazzling virtuosity in their arabesques of sound play and syntax, wordplay and image. It is probably more than a coincidence that the very pinnacle of ancient Hebrew poetry was reached in Job, the biblical text that is most daring and innovative in its imagination of God, man, and creation; for here as elsewhere in the Hebrew Bible the literary medium is not merely a means of "conveying" doctrinal positions but an adventurous occasion for deepening doctrine through the play of literary resources, or perhaps even, at least here, for leaping beyond doctrine.

The facts of the matter, however, are rather more untidy than I have indicated so far. It is our own predisposition to parcel out prose writing into fiction and nonfiction, as is done in our libraries and our lists of best-sellers; and, despite the occasional occurrence of a prose poem, we also tend to think of prose and poetry as distinct, even opposed, categories. For the ancient Hebrews, these were not strict oppositions, and sometimes they could be intertwined in baffling ways. Fiction and nonfiction, because they seem to involve a substantive issue of the truth value of a text, pose a thorny question to which we shall have to return, but from where we stand we probably have no way of recovering what might have figured as a fact in the ancient Hebrew mind, whether the narrative data of centuries-old oral traditions were assumed to be facts, or to what extent the writers consciously exercised a license of invention.

The interplay of poetry and prose is more definable because it is a formal issue, verse being scannable, even the "free rhythms" of biblical parallelistic verse. Some texts, like Psalms, Proverbs, Song of Songs, and all but the frame-story of Job, are unambiguously assemblages of poems, but there are also many mixed instances. Biblical prophecy is composed predominantly in formal verse, but there are also substantial portions of prose prophecy and passages of rhythmic prose that sometimes almost scan. The overwhelming bulk of the narrative books is written in prose, in contrast to the practice of other ancient literatures, but the texture of the prose is studded with verse insets—most often a memorable small set piece just one or two lines long at some particularly significant or ceremonial juncture in the narrative; occasionally, a full-scale poem of fifty or more lines.

This by no means exhausts the formal untidiness of the texts with which we have to deal. For the Hebrew Bible quite frequently incorporates as integral elements of its literary structures kinds of writing that, according to most modern preconceptions, have nothing to do with "literature." I am thinking in particular of genealogies, etiological tales, laws (including the most technical cultic regulations), lists of tribal borders, detailed historical itineraries. Those who view the Bible as literature in conventional terms have quietly ignored these materials as unfortunate encumbrances, while most modern historical scholarship has seen in them either an inscrutable ancient impulse to cherish traditions for their own sake or an effort to provide quasi-documentary authentication for political realities of the later biblical period. As a result, the sundry lists have been analyzed by scholars chiefly for whatever hints of long-lost history they might preserve in fossilized form or for whatever oblique reflections they might offer of the situation of the later writers and redactors.

One need not reject such considerations to argue, as several recent literary students of these texts have persuasively done, that the lists are very effectively employed to amplify the themes and to effect a complementary imaginative realization, in another genre, of the purposes of the narratives in which they are embedded. Thus, J. P. Fokkelman proposes that the abundant genealogies in Genesis are enactments of the theme of propagation and survival so central to that book; David Damrosch invites us to see the laws of the cult in Leviticus as a symbolic realization of an order of wholeness contrasted to the pattern of human failure reiterated in the surrounding narrative; David Gunn suggests that the lists of tribal borders in Joshua are a way of imaginatively mapping out and making real the as yet unconquered Land.[2] In any case, the Hebrew Bible, though it includes some of the most extraordinary narratives and poems in the Western literary tradition, reminds us that literature is not entirely limited to story and poem, that the coldest catalog and the driest etiology may be an effective subsidiary instrument of literary expression.

The evidence of the texts suggests that the literary impulse in ancient Israel was quite as powerful as the religious impulse or, to put it more accurately, that the two were inextricable, so that in order to understand the latter, you have to take full account of the former. In all biblical narrative and in a good deal of biblical poetry as well, the domain in which literary invention and religious imagination are joined is history, for all these narratives, with the exception of Job and possibly Jonah, purport to be true accounts of things that have occurred in historical time. Let us consider one extended example of a text in which historical experience is recast, perhaps even reinvented, in a highly wrought literary art that embodies a religious perspective and also encompasses elements that later conventions would set beyond the pale of literature.

Chapter 11 of Judges recounts the disturbing story of Jephthah's daughter. Jephthah, before going into battle against the Ammonites, makes the imprudent vow that if he returns victorious he will offer to the Lord whoever (or whatever) first comes out from the doors of his house to greet him. In the event, it is his only daughter who comes out, and Jephthah, persuaded that the vow is irrevocable, sacrifices her, first granting her request of a stay of two months, during which she and her maiden friends can "bewail her virginity" (Judg. 11:38). Now, the historical scholars, with some plausibility, view the whole story of the vow and the sacrifice as an etiological tale devised to explain the curious annual custom, mentioned at the end of the chapter, of the daughters of Israel going up into the mountains to lament for four days. We are scarcely in a position to decide on the historical facts of the matter. Perhaps there was a Jephthah who actually sacrificed his daughter (in contravention, of course, of the strictest biblical prohibition), and then a local cult sprang up around the death of the young woman. It may be more likely that in the region of Gilead there was a pagan cult—for the sake of the argument, let us say, of a Persephone-like goddess—which was adopted by the Israelite women; when the origins of these rites had been forgotten, the story was invented to explain them.

We often think of such etiological tales as belonging to the realm of early folk traditions rather than to literature proper, being a "primitive" attempt to explain puzzling realities narratively; and such condescension has frequently been reflected in scholarly treatment of the Bible. But etiological tales are in fact essential elements of many artfully complex and symbolically resonant stories in the Hebrew Bible. The Deluge story culminates in, but can hardly be reduced to, an answer to the etiological question, How did the rainbow get in the sky? The haunting tale of Jacob and the angel (Gen. 32:24–32) is in some way generated by, yet transcends, the question, Why do Israelites refrain from eating the sinew of the animal's thigh? And in Jephthah's story, whatever explanation is provided through the tale for the origins of an obscure practice is subsumed under the more complex literary enterprise of interrelating character, motive, event, historical pattern, political institution, and religious perspective. That art of interrelation is the hallmark of the great chain of narratives that runs from Joshua to 2 Kings.

Let us now look at just the first large segment of the Jephthah story. For reasons that will soon be apparent, the story actually begins with the last two verses of Chapter 10, before the figure of Jephthah is introduced at the beginning of Chapter 11.

CHAPTER 10

17. The Ammonites were mustered, and camped in Gilead. And the Israelites gathered and camped in Mitzpah.
18. And the people, the officers of Gilead, said to one another, "Let the man who will begin to fight against the Ammonites be head of all the inhabitants of Gilead!"

CHAPTER 11

1. Jephthah the Gileadite was an able warrior, and he was the son of a whore. Gilead had begotten Jephthah. 2. And Gilead's wife bore him sons, and the sons of the wife grew up and banished Jephthah. They said to him, "You shall not inherit in our father's house, for you are the son of another woman." 3. Then Jephthah fled from his brothers and settled in the land of Tob, and there gathered round Jephthah worthless fellows who went out raiding with him. 4. And after a time, the Ammonites fought with Israel. 5. And when the Ammonites fought with Israel, the elders of Gilead went to take Jephthah from the land of Tob. 6. And they said to Jephthah, "Come, be our captain so that we can fight against the Ammonites." 7. And Jephthah said to the elders of Gilead, "Why, you hated me, and banished me from my father's house, and can you come to me now when you are in trouble?" 8. And the elders of Gilead said to Jephthah, "For that very reason now we have come back to you, and if you go with us and fight against the Ammonites, you shall be head of all the inhabitants of Gilead." 9. And Jephthah said to the elders of Gilead, "If you bring me back to

fight against the Ammonites, and the Lord delivers them to me, I shall be your head." 10. And the elders of Gilead said to Jephthah, "Let the Lord be witness between us that we will do as you have spoken." 11. Then Jephthah went with the elders of Gilead and the people made him head and captain over them. And Jephthah spoke all his words before the Lord in Mitzpah.

Whether or not things happened precisely as reported here, and whether or not the ancient audience conceived this as a literally accurate account of historical events (both questions are unanswerable), it is clear from the way the text is organized that the writer has exercised considerable freedom in shaping his materials to exert subtle interpretive pressure on the figures and events. In such writing, it is increasingly difficult to distinguish sharply between history and fiction, whatever the historical intentions of the writers. Admittedly, even modern "scientific" historiography has certain rhetorical features, but biblical narrative stands at the far end of the same spectrum, the language of narration and dialogue never being a transparent vehicle to convey the events but constantly standing in the foreground, always intended to be *perceived* as a constitutive element of the events.[3]

The very names and geographical indications in the story, whether they were happily found by the writer in his historical material or contrived for thematic purposes, form part of the pattern of meaning. Jephthah's name means "he will open," a cognate of the verb *patsah* that he uses when he says in anguish to his daughter, "I have opened my mouth unto the Lord" (Judg. 11:35). The eponymous Gilead begets him, almost as though the clan itself begot him, and thus a simple genealogical datum is immediately ironized, for he is expelled by Gilead as a collective entity, then courted by its elders for reasons of frightened self-interest. He gathers around him a band of desperadoes in the land of Tob, which, however real a geographical designation, also means "good" and thus participates in another turn of irony, the land of good being the badlands from which the banished man longs to return to a home.

Jephthah's is a tale of calamitous vow taking, and this initial section constantly plays with vows and pledges and the verbal terms they involve. At their encampment in Mitzpah the Gileadites take a vow that whoever succeeds in leading them against the Ammonites will "be head of all the inhabitants of Gilead." When Jephthah's half brothers decide to drive him out—apparently with the threat of force, for in the next verse we learn that he has to flee—they address him with what amounts to a legal declaration: "You shall not inherit in our father's house, for you are the son of another woman."

It would have been easy enough for the author to report this as interior monologue (as elsewhere in the Bible, "They said in their hearts") or as private speech among the brothers. Instead, his choice of direct discourse addressed to Jephthah (in which the narrator's plain term *whore* is euphemistically veiled by the brothers as "another woman") sharpens the element of confrontation so important in the story and suggests that this is a binding pronouncement of disinheritance meant to be heard by witnesses. The latter suspicion may be confirmed by Jephthah's accusation of the elders, making them accomplices in his banishment ("Why, you hated me, and banished me . . ."). When the elders come to Jephthah, speaking to him quite brusquely (biblical Hebrew is rich in polite forms of address, which they pointedly avoid in their opening words), they renege on the original terms of the collective vow and offer him, instead of the chieftainship over all the inhabitants of Gilead, a mere military command, not "head" but "captain."[4]

As in virtually all one-sided dialogues in the Hebrew Bible, we are invited to wonder about the feelings and motives of the party who remains silent. Jephthah says nothing to his brothers, only flees; but years later, when he receives the rudely pragmatic invitation of the elders, his pent-up resentment emerges: "Why, you hated me . . . and can you come to me now when you are in trouble?" The biblical writers repeatedly use dialogue not merely to define political positions with stylized clarity, as Thucydides does, but also to delineate unfolding relations, nuances of character and attitude. The elders' brusque words trigger Jephthah's outburst. Then, caught out and trying to backpedal rhetorically, they become more voluble and more polite, introducing their remarks with a causal indication, "For that very reason," which doesn't really refer to anything but vaguely seeks to give him the impression that all along they have been seeking to make amends.

Their speech also underlines the thematic key words of *going* and *returning* or *bringing back* (the latter two reflect the same root in the Hebrew), which focus the story of banishment from the house and the flawed attempt of return to the house. This use of what Buber and Rosenzweig first designated as *Leitwort* (on the model of *Leitmotiv*), pervasive in biblical narrative, is still another instance of the flaunted prominence of the verbal medium. At the tragic climax of the story, when Jephthah confesses his vow to his daughter, he says, pathetically, "I cannot go back" (Judg. 11:35).

But the poised choreography of words, in which formulations are pointedly reiterated and internally shifted as they are repeated, is most evident in the changing language of the vow. The elders, having been exposed by Gilead, now revert to the original terms of the vow taken at Mitzpah: "If you go with us, and fight against the Ammonites, you shall be head of all the inhabitants of Gilead." Jephthah accepts these terms, omitting the comprehensive flourish of "all the inhabitants of Gilead" and stipulating that he will assume the leadership only if the Lord grants him victory. Interestingly, it is Jephthah, the banished bastard and guerrilla chieftain, and not the representatives of the Gileadite establishment, who first invokes the Lord. His problem is not one of being a weak monotheist but of conceiving his religious obligations in pagan terms, not finally understanding what the Lord God requireth of him.

The elders respond to the Jephthah's stipulation by making still another vow ("the Lord be witness between us . . ."). When Jephthah reaches the Gileadite encampment—evidently, the one referred to at the beginning of our text, the whole first section of Chapter 11 being a flashback—he is, from what one can make out, spontaneously acclaimed leader by the people, despite his condition to the elders that this should occur only after the victory. They make him "head and captain over them," both president and commander in chief, thus carrying out equally the terms of the initial vow and those of the elders' first offer to Jephthah. The entire section of exposition then closes with still another speech act that is continuous with the string of vows: Jephthah speaks words before the Lord, perhaps not yet the words that will bring disaster on his daughter and himself, but at least an ominous foreshadowing of them.

These interconnecting details of the text at hand then link up with a larger pattern of political themes in Judges and a still larger thematic pattern variously manifested in other narrative books of the Bible. At issue, above all, in Judges is the question of right rule and fitting rulers, the sequence of judges devolving by stages toward the state of general anarchy and civil war represented in the five closing chapters. Unlike Samson, the subject of the next major story in the line, Jephthah has a certain poise and command as a leader: he shows himself, perhaps surprisingly, an able diplomat in his negotiations with the enemy intended to avert war; he is obviously a tough and effective military leader; his exchange with the elders also indicates a quality of shrewdness. But the vow, together with his inflexible adherence to carrying it out, is a fatal flaw, and it is not surprising that after his personal catastrophe he should preside as leader over a bloody civil war (Chapter 12) in which tens of thousands of fellow Israelites perish at the hands of his army. The banishment at the beginning, at the head of a band of desperadoes, looks forward to the David story, but it is the sort of similarity that invites us to contemplate an essential difference: Jephthah is a disastrously more imperfect David who exhibits some of David's gifts but will found no dynasty, build no "house," leave behind him no lasting institutions for national unity.

What can be inferred from all this about the workings of the literary impulse in the Hebrew Bible? Perhaps the most essential point is that literary art is neither intermittent in its exercise nor merely ancillary to the writer's purposes—in this central regard, our passage from the beginning of the Jephthah story is thoroughly characteristic of the whole corpus. To be sure, the writer here is deeply concerned with questions of political leadership, community and individual, the binding nature of vows and pledges, the relationship of father and daughter, man's real and imagined obligations before God; but as a shaper of narrative he engages these complex issues by making constant artful determinations, whether consciously or intuitively, about such matters as the disposition of character, the deployment of dialogue, the attribution or withholding of motives, the use of motifs and thematic key words, the subtle modification of near-verbatim repetition of phrases.

For a reader to attend to these elements of literary art is not merely an exercise in "appreciation" but a discipline of understanding: the literary vehicle is so much the necessary medium through which the Hebrew writers realized their meanings that we will grasp the meanings at best imperfectly if we ignore their fine articulations as literature.

This general principle applies as much to biblical poetry as to prose. A line of Hebrew verse, whether it occurs in a grim denunciation in the Prophets, in an anguished questioning of divine justice in Job, or in the exultation of a psalm of praise, is likely to evince a certain characteristic structure dictated by the formal system of biblical poetry, of which the poets, whatever their spiritual aims, were exquisitely aware. The predominant patterns within the line are in turn associated with a number of characteristic movements for developing the poem as a whole; and some poetic compositions exhibit truly intricate structural features, involving refrainlike devices, strophic divisions, rondo movements, concentric designs, and much else. This is hardly surprising to find in any poetic corpus, but these are not qualities that our usual preconceptions of Scripture have encouraged us to look for in biblical poetry; and, as with the prose, an inattention to the literary medium runs the danger of becoming an inattention to the close weave of meanings.

Let us return briefly to what can be inferred from our illustrative passage specifically about narrative, which remains the dominant genre of the Hebrew Bible. These stories, we generally assume, are part of a religious literature, but that is true only in the rather special sense that virtually every other realm of experience is implicated in the religious perspective. Hence the pungent worldliness of the Hebrew Bible. If what is ultimately at stake in Judges is the possible historical meaning of the ideal of God's kingship over Israel, what we see in the foreground here, as throughout the Hebrew narratives, are issues like the strife between brothers, the struggle over a patrimony, the opposition between legitimate wife and illegitimate mate, the bitterness of personal exile, the lines of political tension in the triangle of individual, community leaders, and populace. The narrator's extreme reticence in telling us what we should think about all these conflicts and questions is extraordinary, and, more than any other single feature, it may explain the greatness of these narratives. Is Jephthah a hero or a villain, a tragic figure or an impetuously self-destructive fool? There are bound to be disagreements among readers, but the writer draws us into a process of intricate, tentative judgment by forcing us to negotiate on our own among such terms, making whatever use we can of the narrative data he has provided.

There are, of course, explicit judgments on particular characters and acts from time to time in biblical narrative: and so-and-so did evil in the eyes of the Lord. But these are no more than exceptions that prove the rule, most frequently occurring in connection with cultic transgressions, as in Kings, with its constant concern about the exclusive claims of the Temple cult in Jerusalem. The general rule that embraces the more characteristic refusal of explicit judgment is the famous laconic quality of biblical narrative. There is never leisurely description for its own sake; scene setting is accomplished with the barest economy of means; characters are sped over a span of years with a simple summary notation until we reach a portentous conjunction rendered in dialogue; and, in keeping with all this, analysis and assessment of character are very rare, and then very brief. We have no idea what Jephthah looks like, what he is wearing, whether he is taller or shorter than his brothers, where they are standing when they pronounce banishment on him; and his feelings about being thrust out can be inferred only from his subsequent words to the elders.

Many of these habits of reticence may be plausibly attributed to an underlying aesthetic predisposition. The masters of ancient Hebrew narrative were clearly writers who delighted in an art of indirection, in the possibilities of intimating depths through the mere hint of a surface feature, or through a few words of dialogue fraught with implication. Their attraction to narrative minimalism was reinforced by their sense that stories should be told in a way that would move efficiently to the heart of the matter, never pausing to elaborate mimetic effects for their own sake. In Homer we are given, for example, a feast of feasts, these daily rituals of hospitality and degustation having an intrinsic allure for the poet and his audience. In the Hebrew Bible, we learn precious little about anyone's menu, and then it usually proves to be for a thematic point. Exceptionally, we are offered some details of the repast Abraham orders for the angels (Genesis 18) because his pastoral hospitality (as against Lot's urban hospitality at the beginning of the next chapter) needs to be underlined. We are told specifically that Jacob is cooking lentil pottage (Genesis 25) when his famished brother comes in from the hunt, so that an emphatic pun can be made on the "red red stuff" of the pottage and Esau's name Edom, the Red. (For a detailed discussion of this episode, see chapter 4.) David's daughter Tamar prepares a delicacy called *levivot* (the identifying recipe has not survived) for her supposedly sick half brother Amnon (2 Sam. 13:8) in order that another, more ironic pun can be introduced: he is in love, or in lust, with her, is in fact about to rape her, and she offers him a kind of food whose name points to the word *lev*, "heart." (For a verb that puns on *lev* in a related way, see Song of Songs 4:9.)

The often drastic reticence of the Hebrew writers led Erich Auerbach, in a famous essay that could be taken as the point of departure for the modern literary understanding of the Bible, to speak of Hebrew narrative as a text "fraught with background."[5] Auerbach, analyzing the somber and troubling story of the Binding of Isaac, was thinking chiefly of the way that the stark surface details bring us to ponder unexpressed psychological depths and theological heights; but in more typical biblical tales, where the perspective is not the vertiginous vertical one between man and God but a broader horizontal overview on the familial, social, erotic, and political interactions among human figures, the crucial consequence of reticence is the repeated avoidance of explicit judgment of the characters. There is, in the view of the Hebrew writers, something elusive, unpredictable, unresolvable about human nature. Man, made in God's image, shares a measure of God's transcendence of categories, images, defining labels. The recourse to implicit judgment opens up vistas of ambiguity—sometimes in matters of nuance, sometimes in essential regards—in our perception of the characters.

Who, for example, is Esau? The midrash, seeing him typologically as the iniquitous Edom-Rome, proposed a black-and-white answer, but the text itself withholds such easy resolution. At first Esau figures as an impetuous hairy oaf, a strong man with a bow but ruled by the growling of his own stomach; then, as a rather pathetic overgrown child weeping to his father over the purloined blessing. But when, with the returning Jacob, we meet Esau again after twenty years, he seems full of princely generosity toward his brother; and though prenatal oracle, sold birthright, and stolen blessing have all confirmed Jacob's preeminence, in their final scene together (Genesis 33) it is Jacob who repeatedly prostrates himself and calls himself "servant" and Esau "master." Does all this somehow cast a retrospective light of ironic qualification on Jacob's promised destiny? Does it suggest that we have at least partly misperceived Esau, or rather that he has grown morally during all those years during which Jacob labored and struggled with Laban in Mesopotamia? (For further consideration of this episode, see pages 205–9.) As elsewhere, we are left wondering about alternatives, feeling that no clear-cut judgment is possible, because the narrator keeps his lips sealed.

Meir Sternberg, who has devoted the most elaborate analysis to biblical procedures for opening up gaps and fostering ambiguities in the stories, makes the apt distinction that ancient Hebrew narrative is ideological but not didactic.[6] The story of Jacob and Esau is an especially instructive case in point. The eponymous second name attached to each of the twins, Israel and Edom, respectively, sets the two up in what one might expect would be a heavily tilted political opposition: the covenanted people over against one of its notorious historical adversaries. But the story itself points toward a rather complicated balance of moral claims in the rivalry, perhaps because the writer, in fleshing out the individual characters, began to pull them free from the frame of reference of political allegory, and perhaps also because this is a kind of ideological literature that incorporates a reflex of ideological auto-critique.

What I have said so far may seem to sidestep a fundamental methodological question that has preoccupied biblical studies for a century and a half: the frequent unreliability of the received text and its accretive evolution through several eras of Israelite history. It is all very well, many biblical critics would still argue, to speak of unities and internal echoes and purposeful ambiguities in a short story by Faulkner or a poem by Wallace Stevens, because one writer was responsible for the text from beginning to end, down to the very proofreading and to any revisions in later editions. But how can we address the patchwork of the biblical text in the same fashion? By what warrant, for example, could I speak of poised ambiguities in the story of Jacob and Esau when scholarship long ago concluded that the tale is a stitching together of three separate "documents" conventionally designated E, J, and P? According to a periodically challenged consensus, the first two of these would have originated in the first two centuries of the Davidic monarchy, probably drawing on still earlier folk traditions, and all three were then cut and pasted to form a single text by anonymous Priestly redactors sometime after the destruction of the First Commonwealth, probably in the sixth or fifth century B.C.E.

I have no quarrel with the courage of conjecture of those engaged in what Sir Edmund Leach has shrewdly called "unscrambling the omelette,"[7] but the essential point for the validity of the literary perspective is that we have in the Bible, with far fewer exceptions than the historical critics would allow, a very well made omelette indeed. Modern biblical scholarship is a product of the post-Gutenberg era, which may be one reason why it is predisposed to conceive authorship in rather narrow and exclusive terms. Collective works of art are not unknown phenomena, as we should be reminded by the medieval cathedrals growing through generations under the hands of successive waves of artisans, or by cinema, where the first-stage work of director, cameraman, and actors achieves its final form in the selection, splicing, and reordering that goes on in the editing room. If in general the literary imagination exhibits what Coleridge called an "esemplastic" power, a faculty for molding disparate elements into an expressively unified whole not achieved outside of art, this power is abundantly evident in the work of the so-called redactors, so the dividing line between redactor and author is often hard to draw or, if it is drawn, does not necessarily demarcate an essential difference.

One important matter that remains undecidable is whether the redactors exercised any freedom in reworking inherited texts, or whether they felt restricted merely to selecting and combining what had been passed on to them. If the latter is true, as many scholars have tended to assume, we must conclude at the very least that the redactors exhibited a genius in creating brilliant collages out of traditional materials, though my own suspicion is that they did not hesitate to change a word, a phrase, perhaps even a whole speech or narrator's report, in order to create precisely the kind of interconnections of structure, theme, and motif to which I have been referring. If literary analysis, with the exception of one recent sectarian manifestation that radically disavows all unities,* is in one way or another a response to the esemplastic activity of the literary imagination, it will not be surprising that the new literary criticism of the Bible has tended to uncover unities where previous biblical scholars, following the hidden imperative *the more atomistic, the more scientific,* found discontinuities, contradictions, duplications, fissures.

The new literary perspective, let me stress, does not come to restore the seamless unitary character of the biblical text cherished by pious tradition, but it does argue in a variety of ways that scholarship, from so much overfocused concentration on the seams, has drawn attention away from the design of the whole. Thus, some of the new literary analysts of the Bible simply set aside any consideration of hypotheses about the composite origins of the text because they find other issues more productive to discuss. (By and large, that has been my own predisposition.) Others, like James Ackerman, David Damrosch, and Leslie Brisman, explicitly use scholarly opinion about disparate elements in the text in order to see how once independent units are given new meanings and contribute to the formation of larger patterns of meaning, by having been placed where they are in the final text continuum. In either case, the goal is to lead us toward what the biblical authors and author-redactors surely aimed for—a continuous *reading* of the text instead of a nervous hovering over its various small components.

Another difficulty, however, remains: quite frequently in the Hebrew Bible we may not have a dependable text to read.

---

*The notion that every text is divided against itself is a fundamental dogma of the critical school known as deconstruction, which began in Paris in the late 1960s and became fashionable in America and England a decade later.

The oldest texts of single biblical books or parts of books are, as I noted earlier, preserved in the sectarian Dead Sea Scrolls, several centuries after the original composition. The oldest integral manuscript of the Hebrew Bible is a whole millennium later. Ancient witnesses beginning with the Septuagint sometimes provide help in difficult places, but their variants of the Masoretic text often reflect glosses, misunderstandings, or dubious textual traditions. There are certainly no grounds for confidence that the Bible we have is exactly the one produced by the original writers, though the degree of textual difficulties varies sharply. For long stretches of Genesis, Exodus, and other narrative books, the text seems relatively clean, with only an occasional local problem; in Job and in some of the poetic sections of the Prophets, there are lines and occasionally even passages that are only barely intelligible.

Most of these difficulties appear to be textual, though some are merely philological, for poetry—and in the Bible, Job above all—mines lexical resources not used elsewhere, involving terms whose meaning is uncertain. Comparative Semitic philology has made impressive progress in recovering many of these lost meanings and, in the case of more common words and idioms, in giving us a more precise sense of denotations and connotations. Since literary analysis needs at some level to respond to the nuances of words, the advances in biblical philology over the past several decades have been a necessary precondition for the development of the new literary criticism of the Bible that began to emerge in the 1970s. There are words and phrases and verses that will remain dark spots on the map, whether for philological or textual reasons, but by and large the Hebrew text is now more accessible to understanding than it has been for the past two thousand years.

Let me propose that, conversely, the application of properly literary analysis to the Bible is a necessary precondition to a sounder textual scholarship. At the beginning of his narratological study of Deuteronomy, Robert Polzin argues for "an operational priority to literary analysis at the preliminary stages of research."[8] If I may unpack that somewhat forbidding social-scientific formulation, the basic methodological issue is this: before you can decide whether a text is defective, composite, or redundant, you have to determine to the best of your ability the formal principles on which the text is organized. These are by no means the same for all times and places, as the nineteenth-century German founders of modern biblical scholarship often imagined.

One has only to scan the history of a recent literary genre, the novel, to see how rapidly formal conventions shift, and to realize that elements like disjunction, interpolation, repetition, and contrastive styles, which in biblical scholarship were long deemed sure signs of a defective text, may be perfectly deliberate components of the literary artwork, and recognized as such by the audience for which it is intended. There is a distinctive poetics informing both biblical narrative and biblical poetry, and an understanding of it will help us in many instances to make plain sense of a puzzling text instead of exercising that loose and derivative mode of literary invention that goes under the scholarly name of emendation.

A couple of examples should clarify the methodological point. In Proverbs 7:9, in the introductory movement of the vivid narrative poem about the gullible young man and the dangerous seductress, we are told that he goes out into the streets, where she is waiting to meet him, "At twilight, as evening falls, / in pitch-black night and darkness." This line of verse has troubled some textual scholars because it seems a violation of logic. If it is twilight, how can it be pitch-black night? When one adds that the Hebrew word 'ishon that I have rendered as "pitch-black" usually means the dark, or apple, of the eye and occurs in verse 2 ("let my teaching be like the apple of your eye"), we have both crux and solution.

The ancient scribe, nodding, inadvertently repeated in verse 9 the word *'ishon,* which belonged only in verse 2. Then someone added "in darkness" as a gloss. What must be done to "restore" the text is to erase the whole second verset of this line and attach the first verset to the next line.

But if one considers precisely how lines of biblical poetry are generally constructed, the purported crux dissolves and the whole procedure of emendation becomes gratuitous. For it can readily be shown that in many hundreds of lines in the biblical corpus, the relation between the first verset and the second is *narrative:* under the umbrella of parallelism or overlapping meaning that covers the two halves of the line, the second action or image follows in time after the first. Our line from Proverbs, then, is not a break with logic but a particularly striking instance of a general principle of poetic logic observable in biblical verse: in one instant, we see the young man setting out into the streets at twilight; in the next instant, it is already totally dark, a suitable cover for the seductress as she marks her sexual target. This little temporal jump between versets may even be grounded in a mimesis of nature, for sunsets in the eastern Mediterranean seem to happen very quickly; and we should also note that the seductress's reference later, in verse 20, to a full moon evidently a couple of weeks off indicates that the action of the poem takes place at the dark of the moon. As for the occurrence of *'ishon* in verse 9, this makes perfect sense in terms of another principle of biblical poetics—the practice of tying together distinct segments of the poem (here, the framing introductory lines and then the narrative body of the poem) through the repetition of some prominent word, whether in the identical sense or in a play on two different senses. Again, this is a formal organizing principle that can be demonstrated analytically in scores of examples. Thus, in reading the poem more fully through an awareness of its poetics, we also come to see why it is absurd to rewrite the text in order to make it conform to a logic alien to it.

Let us consider one example of a supposedly defective narrative text, the first verses of 2 Samuel 5, which report David's confirmation as king over all the tribes of Israel after the conclusion of the civil war with the tribes supporting the house of Saul.

> All the tribes of Israel came to David at Hebron and said, "Here, we are your bone and flesh. Long ago, when Saul was king over us, you were Israel's leader in battle. And the Lord said to you:
>   You shall shepherd my people
>   and you shall be ruler over Israel."
> All the elders of Israel came to the king at Hebron, and King David made a covenant with them in Hebron before the Lord, and they anointed David king over Israel.

The apparent difficulty here is that the last sentence is a repetition of the first. The atomistic solution of some textual scholars runs along the following lines. Two traditions, using similar formulations, have been rather clumsily spliced together by the editor: in the first tradition, it was the tribes of Israel who came to Hebron; in the second tradition, the elders. Thus, the editorial compulsion to incorporate both traditions introduced a redundancy as well as a contradiction in the text. This is another instance in which inattention to the organizing literary principles of the text leads to faulty scholarship. The Hebrew writers frequently use a framing technique that in fact biblical scholars have identified and designated *resumptive repetition:* if the progress of a narrative line is interrupted by some digression or specification, the writer marks the return to the point where the main line was left by repeating the statement made just before the interruption.

Our passage proves to be a rather subtle adaptation of this

general technique. In the first instance, a popular movement acclaiming David worthy of kingship is recorded. "All the tribes of Israel" come to him, and their support is represented by quotation of their speech, in which is embedded a quotation on their part of divine speech—appropriately, it has the solemnity of a line of formal verse—that is an explicit promise to David of the role of leader. After these two pieces of direct discourse, the resumptive repetition takes us back to the initial narrative statement before the dialogue and continues with a summary of the political act that was consummated at Hebron. This time, however, the elders rather than the tribes are singled out as agents because, although it may be the prerogative of the populace to acclaim, it is the prerogative of the elders formally to confirm David's kingship in the ceremony of anointment.

We should also note that in the initial report the tribes come to "David" and in the concluding report the elders come to "the king," who is then immediately referred to as "King David," both terms being proleptic of the end of the sentence, in this way underscoring the binding force of the anointment. The actual term *king* appears in the quoted discourse of the tribes only in retrospective reference to Saul, but God's words promising that David will be "ruler [*nagid*] over Israel" are picked up by the narrator at the end and given an unambiguous political definition when David is anointed "king [*melekh*] over Israel." Thus, the technique of resumptive repetition has been joined with a still more common technique of biblical prose, minute focusing through small variations in near-verbatim repetition.[9] The supposedly composite and redundant text turns out to be a tightly woven unit in which repetition is used to frame the central dialogue and sharpen the political theme.

If the arguments I have been laying out suggest why a literary approach to the Hebrew Bible is fully warranted and in

certain ways required by the nature of the material, they omit
still another complicating consideration—the diachronic
dimension of this literary corpus. Here, again, there is a difference between the Hebrew Bible and the New Testament that
is both quantitative and qualitative. The New Testament,
reflecting a particular portentous moment in history, is the
work of a few generations; the Hebrew Bible spans nearly a
millennium of literary activity. How much did Hebrew literature change over this period, which covers about as much
time as elapsed in French literature from the *Song of Roland* to
the novels of Alain Robbe-Grillet? In poetry, the changes are
surprisingly minor, having to do more with certain features of
grammatical forms and diction than with any underlying shift
in notions of poetic style and structure.

It is true that the earliest poetic texts, such as the Song of
Deborah, exhibit a fondness for incantatory movements and
incremental repetition that are not often found in later poems,
but the formal system of versification and basic conceptions
about the poetic medium do not change substantively over
this whole long period. Job, the supreme poetic achievement
of the era after the destruction of the First Commonwealth,
probably reflects its historical moment in the abundant borrowing from Aramaic in its vocabulary, but poetically it is
perfectly continuous with the poetic creations of the First
Commonwealth; any formal differences are attributable to the
individual genius of the poet or to the generic aims of the
genre of radical Wisdom literature for which he made his
verse a vehicle. A very late book, Ecclesiastes (fourth or third
century B.C.E.), does move toward a new horizon of literary
form but, instructively, does so by abandoning the system of
parallelistic verse for a kind of cadenced prose that incorporates small pieces of verse, a good many of them wry parodies
of Proverbs.

In narrative, on the other hand, despite some strong elements of continuity, new styles and new notions of narrative art emerge in the post-Exilic period. The golden age of Hebrew narrative was the First Commonwealth era, when the great sequence of works from Genesis to Kings was given its initial formulation. The brilliantly laconic style, with its uncanny ability to intimate psychological and thematic complexities (one has only to think of the story of Joseph and his brothers, or the David story), came to full flowering during this period. Certain features of this classic narrative art, like the use of thematic key words and refrain-like repetitions, are still observable in a late tale like Jonah, and if the Book of Ruth, whose dating is still disputed, is in fact late, then it represents an extraordinary archaizing redeployment of the earlier conventions.

But from the perspective of literary history, most of the new Hebrew narratives created after 586 B.C.E. are distinctly the products of a postclassical age. Instead of one dominant form, as in the earlier period, there is a proliferation of forms, perhaps a kind of experimentation with different forms by different writers over nearly four centuries of the post-Exilic period. Ezra-Nehemiah and Chronicles represent new strategies for the narrative engagement of history through autobiographical writing, annalistic recapitulation, the buttressing of the report of history through personal observation or, alternatively, through the citation of sources.

Jonah, Esther, and Daniel, in quite different ways, depart from the general norm of historical and psychological realism that, despite the occasional intervention of divine agency or miraculous event, governs classical Hebrew narrative. Jonah has variously been described as a parable, a Menippean satire, or a sailor's yarn, and it is clear that the writer has stretched the contours of reality with a zestful overtness to suit his ends, not only in the famous instance of Jonah's descent into the belly of the big fish but also in such details as the dimensions of Nineveh (at three days' walk, it would be much bigger than Los Angeles) and the animals that are made to fast and don sackcloth. Daniel, in its insistent theme of piety (the classic Hebrew narratives are religious but never quite pious in this way), its intimations of an apocalypse, and some of its formal structures, is closely akin to certain texts of the Apocrypha, and very much a work of the Hellenistic period. Esther, though it purportedly represents events in the Persian imperial court in Susa, takes place in a fairy-tale never-never land where, for example, a parade of all the fairest maidens of the kingdom is brought to the royal bed night after night, each beauty having been exquisitely prepared for the king's delectation by being soaked six months in oil of myrrh and another six in assorted perfumes. There is broad comedy here of a sort absent from the earlier narratives, and also a rather simple didacticism not found in First Commonwealth writing. The stringent narrative economy of the classical literature has been replaced by a reveling in the sumptuousness of details of milieu, often cast in the form of descriptive catalog: "There were white cotton and blue wool hangings, fastened with cords of fine linen and purple wool to silver rings and pillars of alabaster: the beds were of gold and silver upon a floor of marble, alabaster, mother-of-pearl, and carnelian" (Esther 1:6). We need not invoke a direct influence from the Greek sphere to detect here the beginnings of a Hebrew literature that is heading toward Hellenistic horizons.

We have seen, then, that there is striking variety in the body of ancient Hebrew literature preserved in the Bible, a variety that stems from the long centuries through which it evolved, the different genres it represents, the divergent aims and viewpoints of its authors. All that notwithstanding, this is a corpus that bears within it the seeds of its own canonicity. Earlier, we noted the strong elements of internal allusion in Hebrew Scripture that at many points make it a set of texts in restless dialogue with one another. In the end, this is something that goes beyond what is ordinarily thought of in strictly literary terms as intertextuality.

Although I think it is inaccurate to speak, as some have done, of a "system" of symbols in the Hebrew Bible, it is clear that the various texts exploit certain recurrent symbols which, however dictated by the topography, geography, history, and climate of ancient Israel, become a unifying way of conceiving the world, of referring the discrete data of historical and individual experience to large interpretive patterns. (This degree of symbolic cohesiveness among the Hebrew texts in turn helped make them assimilable into the new symbolic framework of the New Testament.) Thus, the act of dividing between heaven and earth, water and dry land, which is the initial definition of God's cosmogonic power, proliferates into a whole spectrum of antithetical oppositions: garden or oasis and wasteland, later recurring as Promised Land and Wilderness, or, in another variant, homeland ("the Lord's inheritance") and exile, in either case often with a necessary rite of passage through water to get from one to the other; Israel and the nations; and even calendrically, the Sabbath and the six days of labor. Or, in a pattern less grounded in nature or history than in a concept, the stark initiating act of creation through divine speech from formlessness, chaos, nothingness (*tohu-bohu*) lingers in the Hebrew imagination as a measure of the absoluteness of God's power and also as a looming perspective on the contingency of all human existence and the frailty of all human exercises of knowledge and power. Although, as we have observed, there is ideological debate among the Hebrew writers, this fundamental perception is shared by all (only Ecclesiastes gives it a negative twist), and it is a central instance in which a persistent set of images also is a persistent vision of reality.

A particularly memorable example is the poem about God as transcendent weigher of all creation, composed by the anonymous prophet of the Babylonian Exile referred to by scholars as Deutero-Isaiah (Is. 40:12–26). It would be a great poem even in isolation, but its actual richness has much to do with its ramified connections with the larger context of the Hebrew Bible. (Verses 19 and 20, which depict the foolish activity of artisans making idols, are omitted because they involve several textual difficulties and in any case are not essential to the general point I want to illustrate.)

> *Who with his hand's hollow measured the waters,*
> *the heavens who gauged with a span,*
> *And meted earth's dust with a measure,*
> *weighed with a scale the mountains,*
> *the hills with a balance?*
> *Who has plumbed the spirit of the Lord,*
> *what man has told him his plan?*
> *With whom did he counsel, who taught him,*
> *who led him in the path of right and told him wisdom's*
> *way?*
> *Why, the nations are a drop from the bucket,*
> *like the balance's dust they're accounted,*
> *why, the coastlands he plucks up like motes.*
> *Lebanon is not fuel enough,*
> *its beasts not enough for the offering.*
> *All nations are as naught before him,*
> *he accounts them as empty and nothing.*
> *And to whom would you liken God,*
> *what likeness for him propose?*
> . . . .
> *Do you not know,*
> *have you not heard?*
> *Was it not told you from the first,*
> *have you not understood the foundations of earth?*
> *He's enthroned on the rim of the earth,*
> *and its dwellers are like grasshoppers.*

He spread the heavens like gauze,
    stretched them like a tent to dwell in.
He turns princes into nothing,
    the rulers of earth he makes naught.
Hardly planted, hardly sown,
    hardly their stem rooted in earth—
when he blows on them and they wither,
    the storm bears them off like straw.
"And to whom will you liken me that I be equal?"
    says the Holy One.
Lift up your eyes on high,
    and see, who created these?
He who musters their host by number,
    each one he calls by name.
Through great strength and mighty power
    no one lacks in the ranks.

The poem not only involves the general idea of God as powerful creator but also alludes to a series of key terms from the first account of creation in Genesis. The sequence water-heaven-earth in the three initial versets recalls the three cosmic spheres with which God works on the first three days of the creation. The reiterated assertion that there is no likeness (*demut*) that man can possibly find for God is, of course, a sound argument against idolatry, something that explicitly concerns the prophet; but the term also echoes, by way of ironic inversion, the first creation of humankind: "Let us make man in our image, after our likeness [*demuteinu*]" (Gen. 1:26). That is to say, God is perfectly free to fashion a human creature in his own likeness, but it is utterly beyond the creature's capacity to fashion a likeness for his creator. In a related way, the background of cosmogony is present in the poet's assertion that nations and rulers are as naught, or nothing, before God, since one of the repeated pair of terms in these two sets of lines is *tohu*, the very void out of which the world was first called into being.

Still another ironic crossover between human and divine is effected through an allusion to a different text. To God who is enthroned (or simply "seated") on the rim of the earth, all its inhabitants (the same word in the Hebrew as "he who sits" at the beginning of the line) seem like grasshoppers. This simile links up with the fearful report of the majority of the spies sent by Moses to investigate the land (*'erets*, the same term that here means "earth"). They were dismayed by the enormous size of "its inhabitants" (the same word as in the line we are considering), calling them "people of vast proportions" or, more literally, "people of measure" (*midot*, the same root that is reflected in the verb which begins our poem), "and we were in our own sight as grasshoppers, and so we were in their sight" (Num. 13:33). In short, the grotesque, and inaccurate, simile used by the spies in a reflex of fear here becomes an accurate gauge of the disproportion between creator and creatures, or, indeed, a kind of cosmic understatement.

The essential point, however, is not the prophet's clever use of allusion but the deep affinity of perception with his predecessors that his use of allusion reflects. Despite the network of reminiscences of Genesis (to which the mention of the host of the heavens at the end should be added), the dominant imagery of the poem is actually technological, in part as a rejoinder to the paltry technology of idol making that the poet denounces. God weighs, measures, gauges, and plumbs, but these activities cannot operate in the opposite direction: no man can plumb the unfathomable spirit of the Lord. To set this for a moment in relation to the poet's craft, the person who shaped these lines had a sense of familiarity with the concrete activities of quotidian reality, surveying and architecture and the weighing of merchandise, the cultivation of young plants, and the pitching of tents. The literature of ancient Israel, even in sublime moments like this one, scarcely ever loses this feeling of rootedness in the concrete realities of the here and now.

At the same time, the loftiness of perspective of the poem by Deutero-Isaiah is breathtaking: "He's enthroned on the rim of the earth, / and its dwellers are like grasshoppers." The Hebrew writers in both poetry and prose were deeply engaged by the fate of nations, the destinies of individuals, and the elaborate grid of political institutions and material instrumentalities in which both were enmeshed. The contrast of perspectives that is the explicit subject of our poem is in the narratives often only implicit; but however closely the human scene is followed, there is always a potential sense, perhaps even hinted at in the challenging terseness of the narrative mode of presentation, that merely human aspirations shrink to nothing under the vast overarching aspect of eternity. One measure of the centrality of this vision to the Hebrew imagination is that the imagery and theme of our poem by Deutero-Isaiah, especially in the opening five lines, are strikingly similar to the language of the Voice from the Whirlwind, though in other respects Job (who was perhaps even a near-contemporary) reflects a much more unconsoling view of God and man, at the other end of the spectrum of Israelite thought.

Sometime in the latter part of the second millennium B.C.E., the spiritual avant-garde of the Hebrew people began to imagine creation and creator, history and humankind, in a radically new way. This radicalism of vision, though it would never produce anything like unanimity, generated certain underlying patterns of literary expression in the centuries that followed. In poetry, these were realized technically through a heightening and refinement of formal conventions largely inherited from an antecedent Syro-Palestinian tradition of verse. In the prose narratives, one may infer that these patterns became the very matrix of an extraordinary new kind of representation of action, character, speech, and motive. In both cases, the imaginative recurrence, for all the manifest diversity, to the bedrock assumptions of biblical monotheism about the nature of reality weaves tensile bonds among the disparate texts. This endlessly fascinating anthology of ancient Hebrew literature was also, against all plausible acceptations of the word, on its way to becoming a book.

CHAPTER 4

Narrative Specification
and the Power
of the Literal

O ne of the happier consequences of the renewed literary scrutiny to which the Bible has been subjected over the past decade is that it has brought home in a fresh way an important but half-forgotten truth about Western culture: that the very presuppositions by which we read, our expectations of what literature can do, are predetermined by the decisive early model of the Bible. It is fairly obvious that this should be the case for our institutions of interpretation because, in a network of cultures spun out over two millennia within the orbits of Jewish and Christian faith, the Bible has always been the text par excellence to be interpreted, the object of endless homiletical and philological ingenuity, the occasion for codifying whole systems of hermeneutical principles. If students of literature, philosophy, and intellectual history have been increasingly concerned with the problematic conditions of interpretation and with the elusive processes by which texts prompt or produce meanings, it is hardly surprising that a good deal of recent attention has been devoted to the history of the interpretation of the Bible. People concerned with issues of literary theory are with growing frequency prepared to imagine that there may be more to be learned from watching Augustine or Rabbi Ishmael attempt to untie a knotty verse in Genesis than from watching, let us say, Julia Kristeva ponder an enigmatic sonnet by Mallarmé.

If, however, the new literary approaches to the Bible have reminded us of how the Bible is implicated in the institutions of interpretation, they have also enabled us to see more clearly how the cunning literary articulations of the Bible generated those institutions and in certain ways formed Western notions of what literature was. The most extreme statement of such a perception is the view proposed—with characteristic provocative immoderation—by the maverick Yale critic Harold Bloom in *The Book of J*. In Bloom's view, J, the conjectured author of the oldest continuous narrative strand in the Hebrew Bible, did nothing less than fix the methods by which human nature would be represented in Western literature for the next twenty-five hundred years—until the advent of Shakespeare, who, in part building on J, brought literary representation to a new level of complexity. It is not clear to me how such a claim might be demonstrated, especially since Bloom is rather vague about actual modes of representation, contenting himself with the invocation of more or less Nietzschean terms like *irony, playfulness,* and *vitalism*. In any case, I myself would be inclined to put forth analogous claims for Sophocles, Euripides, and even Homer as the shapers of powerful modes for the representation of human fate and human nature that would prove to be determinative in the work of innumerable later writers, down to our own time.

The Bible is but one of two matrices of our double-edged,

pagan-monotheistic, Hellenic-Hebraic culture. The kernel of valuable insight in Bloom's exaggeration is that it reminds us that there is grave distortion in the common practice of dividing up Greek and Hebrew origins into literature (and philosophy and science) on the Greek side and something called "religion" on the Hebrew side. The system of genres of Western literature is surely of Greek origin, but the narrative imagination of individual human lives caught in a vortex of private motives and dangerous historical forces also begins quite remarkably in the body of texts created at the Hebrew end of the Mediterranean. I suppose the most influential modern critic to insist on this idea was Erich Auerbach, in the still seminal comparison between the *Odyssey* and Genesis with which he began his *Mimesis* (1946). Auerbach stressed the background-fraught spareness of biblical narrative both as the key to the sense of depth in its representation of reality and as the explanation for the endless interpretation the Bible has engendered. In an effort to see what it is about biblical narrative that might offer one model for how literary texts work in our culture, what they invite us to do with them as we read, I would like to propose an emphasis complementary to Auerbach's—not on the looming background and the deliberately yawning gaps in the narrative report but on the actual details in the foreground.

The Bible is famous, or perhaps notorious, for eliciting multiple "levels" of interpretation, for inviting readers to turn it into a figure or allegory of something other than what meets the eye. But is there some way in which the literal force of the narrative details is crucial in the experience of reading? Indeed, one might argue that a general—though by no means uniform—effect of the new literary criticism of the Bible has been to encourage a new, subtle appreciation of the density of the literal in the Bible, as books by Meir Sternberg, David Gunn, Robert Polzin, and Adele Berlin, to mention just a few admirable instances, have variously shown. Perhaps at this moment it is becoming feasible, after two millennia of figurative readings, to think about the "literal meaning" of the Bible. Nothing in a literary text, of course, is more notoriously elusive than literal meaning. In the case of the Bible, the foundational instance for Western culture, there are probably millions of believers across the globe who deem it a spiritual necessity to hew to the literal meaning, while virtually every historian of interpretation and every literary theorist will argue that literal meanings always dissolve into figurative ones, plain sense into allegories, *peshat*—to invoke the rabbinic terminology—into *derash*.

The difficulties of getting hold of the literal have been nicely sorted out by Frank Kermode in his judicious essay "The Plain Sense of Things."[1] Beginning with a poem by Wallace Stevens and then surveying the history of Bible interpretation, Kermode points to three general circumstances of reading that tend to push us away from the literal: the inherent proclivity of the mind for metaphor; the pressure exerted by context, or what some linguists prefer to call co-text; and the pressure of authoritative institutions of interpretation. I will concentrate here on the second of these three complicating circumstances of reading—that is, the relation of any given moment in a text to the texts that immediately and proximately surround it. As Kermode observes, this ultimately leads to the difficult question of the identity of the whole to which the part belongs, the shifting contours of the canon, though our own considerations need not take us so far. The metaphorizing habits of the mind are also to some degree implicated in the issue of co-text because we would not be inclined to see analogies, antitheses, or subterranean correspondences between texts were it not for our predisposition to grasp things through similitude.

The consideration of authority in interpretation, though

paramount for both Christian and Jewish tradition, would seem to be no more than vestigially pertinent to modern secular readers, and perhaps to many modern religious readers as well. Apart from religious fundamentalists and certain intellectual sectarians within the academic world, few readers today look to an institution or authoritative figure that will serve as arbiter of interpretation, fixing its rules and procedures and licit range of application. What we share as interpreters in place of such authority are certain tacit or explicit preferences dictated by the spirit of the age—like the fondness for the concrete (which in fact will inform much of my own argument) that can be related to the modern attachment to archaeology as model and metaphor for grasping the past; and like the postmodern avidness for any kind of reading that will destabilize or multiply meanings.

A rigorously strict construction of literal interpretation is bound to turn it into an impossibility. Every attempt, that is, to reduce the text to a kind of zero degree of meaning, where the textual detail means nothing but itself, finally collapses because, given the pull of co-texts and the allure of metaphor, it is always theoretically possible to conceive meanings beyond the zero degree. Roland Barthes's influential essay from the late 1960s, "The Reality Effect," is a highly sophisticated effort to rescue the absolute literal and thus is a particularly instructive failure.[2] Barthes, looking at the presence in realist prose of all sorts of adventitious or superfluous details—his parade example is the barometer over the piano in Flaubert's *Un Coeur simple*—proposes that they represent "a resistance to meaning" in the text and that through such details "it is the category of the 'real,' and not its various contents, which is being signified."

This intriguing proposal does suggest something about the project of realism in nineteenth-century prose, but the formulation is too pat. Flaubert's barometer as a token of taste, decor, and class already begins to point toward horizons of sociological meaning beyond its sheer concreteness. An implement of technology and a visible index of coming weather, it invites the perception of thematic connections with the story of Félicité, and some readers may also be inclined to see correspondences with other material objects or even events in the story. Thus, in the easiest reflex of readerly imagination, the plain sense of the thing begins to waver, and the barometer threatens to become, alas, a metaphor. To consider for a moment opposite poles of realism, one can say that what is flamboyantly explicit in Balzac is artfully implicit in Flaubert: I am thinking of Balzac's great catalogs of bric-a-brac, his interior scenes and overviews of neighborhoods, in which the narrator insists on the interanimated connection among material details and their links to what is happening in the narrative.

If the prospect of an absolutely nonsymbolic, nonallegorical sense is illusory, we may still speak of textual details that are to be taken literally, that "mean" themselves, whatever else they may mean. The *sensus historicus* that biblical interpretation identifies in Scripture may help us understand how such literal meaning works. Every narrative that purports to be historical presents its details first of all because they "really" happened. The Israelites in the Book of Joshua cross the Jordan into Canaan because that is the route they really followed—or certainly, the route the writer believed they followed—in the thirteenth century B.C.E. Let me hasten to add that the historicity of this crossing in no way impedes the writer from setting it into a framework of symbolic meaning, as the acts and language of the early chapters of Joshua draw repeated analogies to the crossing of the Sea of Reeds in Exodus, thus marking the liminal realm of the wilderness by two barriers of water, the first the threshold from bondage and the second the entrance into the Promised Land. I would propose that even manifestly fictional narratives may be said to possess a *sensus quasi historicus*. In the invented world of *Tom Jones*, the hero "really" travels from his native country estate to London, and the literal factuality of that movement is an essential part of our experience of the story, however much the novelist also represents town and country as thematically antithetical spheres.

We may get a better sighting of this elusive subject by taking a clue from Roland Barthes and focusing on the role of seemingly extraneous narrative detail. Even the most urgently symbolic narratives are filled with insistently literal presences that shape the reader's imaginative experience of the story. Here, for example, are the first sentences of Kafka's *The Castle*, arguably the archetypal modern symbolic novel and the last sustained production of a writer whose work, according to Gershom Scholem, most profoundly resembles the Bible in compelling endless interpretation.

> It was late in the evening when K. arrived. The village was deep in snow. The Castle was hidden, veiled in mist and darkness, nor was there even a glimmer of light to show that a castle was there. On the wooden bridge leading from the main road to the village, K. stood for a long time gazing into the illusory emptiness above him.[3]

The novel's central themes of dubious knowledge and authority, the problematic correspondence of lower and higher realms, are already strongly engaged here: can the Castle ever be seen; is it really there or only a mirage hiding "illusory emptiness"? Yet the sheer literalness of the initial narrative data is not to be dismissed. It is winter and dark and misty, so even if there should be a lit castle somewhere up above, the newcomer, peering up from the village, can see nothing at all. The conjunction of K.'s visual perspective, topography, time of evening, and seasonal weather is perfectly realistic.

In any case, the Castle swathed in mist and darkness is thematically marked, but what about the bridge? I once heard the eminent literary theorist Benjamin Harshav rather impishly ask a very bright graduate student on an oral examination why the bridge at the beginning of *The Castle* was wooden. Taken by surprise, she fumbled, then made a hasty effort to construct a thematic interpretation of the wooden bridge. But no, Harshav interrupted, he merely meant to suggest that the wooden bridge was there because such villages in Central Europe often had wooden bridges, and one wasn't obliged to say it *meant* anything. It is, I think, an instructive instance. Even a novel like *The Castle* that has been such an endlessly resilient springboard for allegorical readings has a certain momentum of immediacy driven by a mimetic impulse. It would be foolhardy to claim that it is impossible for anyone to find symbolic or at least incipiently metaphorical significance in the material composition of Kafka's wooden bridge, but first of all, and also most plausibly, it is a datum of the *sensus quasi historicus* of the novel—it is "in fact" what K. stands on the evening he arrives at the village, before he walks on to find a place at the inn.

The Bible provides particularly fertile ground for a consideration of narrative specification and literal meaning because, by the standard of later European narrative, it is so parsimonious in specification: Abraham may mention a sandal latch in his parlay with Melchisedek as an idiomatic token for something of minimal material value, but no one in the whole biblical corpus is ever described as having a frayed or missing or dangling or firmly tied sandal latch. When a detail of dress, or physical appearance, or cuisine, or agency and action, is introduced in ancient Hebrew narrative, one can reasonably

assume that it is there for a special purpose of thematic assertion or concatenation of plot, though this is not always self-
evidently so. Why do we have to be told that David was
redheaded or ruddy, *'admoni*? Perhaps simply so that he will
catch Goliath's eye and elicit an added edge of contempt as a
conspicuous pretty boy, or perhaps, again, because the *sensus
historicus* required it, because the real David was known for
his hair color or complexion.

One class of narrative specification in the Bible gives the
appearance of being easily accounted for—the instances in
which either the narrator or one of the characters proposes an
explicit reason for the introduction of the detail. Even in such
cases, however, there is generally more at issue in the narrative function of the detail than the flatly stated etiology or
causal relation or moral theme. Let us consider a rare and
famous glimpse into the contents of an ancient Near Eastern
pot—Jacob's lentil stew, which he uses to purchase the
birthright from Esau (Gen. 25:29–34). At first, we are simply
told it is a stew (*nazid*), and the added information that it is
lentil stew is conveyed at the end of the episode (verse 34).
Jacob is cooking lentil stew rather than, say, onion and garlic
stew because the color has to be red. Red-haired or ruddy
Esau looks at the steaming pot and says, "Let me cram my
maw with this red-red [*ha'adom ha'adom hazeh*]," too inarticu-
late to recall in his hunger or his sheer boorishness the ordinary Hebrew word *nazid*, "stew." The narrator seizes Esau's
phrase as an etiological clue, "therefore is he called Edom,"
thus polemically associating the name of a traditional enemy
of Israel with a moment of crude ignorance and foolish impa-
tience. At this point, some readers might be tempted to conclude that we have already lost the literal meaning of Jacob's
stew: the lentils are not plain lentils but a ruddy symbol—
'adom—of the national character of Edom manifested in the
boorish appetite of its eponymous founder. But before we

give up on the literal meaning, we must recognize that figurative meanings by no means stop with the narrator's flat declaration. The testimony of astute readers through the ages is instructive.

Rashi, seconded by other medieval Hebrew exegetes, imagines that Esau has come back from the fields exhausted by the murders he has committed. His initial clue for an interpretation that may be surprising to modern readers is the word `ayef,` "famished," or elsewhere, "faint" or "weary," in which he detects an echo of Jeremiah 4:31: "My soul faints for the killers." This is a prime instance of Frank Kermode's point that the perception of the whole determines the meaning of the part. Rashi, seeing Genesis and Jeremiah as elements of a single grand structure of meaning, quite naturally reads the latter as a gloss on the former. There is, moreover, a still larger canon behind Rashi's reading, one that extends to Midrash and Talmud, in which Edom is understood typologically as Rome, the so-called Wicked Kingdom, whose notorious vocation is murder. But the biblical text itself contains a verbal and phonetic hint that might also trigger this grim reading. Red is, of course, the color of blood, and it may not be inappropriate to hear in Esau's 'adom 'adom a half echo of dam dam, "blood, blood."

Why should Jacob be cooking at all? This domestic activity contrasts him, as a "dweller of tents," with his hunter brother, and in this connection, the fact that he is preparing a vegetarian dish, or at least one in which a legume predominates, intimates something about his character in contradistinction to that of his twin, who prospers from the kill. A 1742 Hebrew commentary, 'Or Hahaim, shrewdly suggests a causal connection between Jacob's puttering around the kitchen and the immediately preceding narrative report that Isaac loved Esau for providing him game: "For, seeing that Esau's mouthful had its effect on Isaac, he too took up cooking dishes as a means to draw his father's heart toward him, as Esau had done." The effect of the immediately adjacent co-text on the text under scrutiny is to complicate the force of the narrative specification. Jacob is cooking lentils—poor fellow, he has no access to succulent venison—not merely to provide a clue for the name Edom but because he desperately wants his father's affection, which has been seen to be bizarrely determined by concerns of cuisine. In this light, the stew is a characterizing fact for Jacob as well as for Esau, a focal point of frustrated filial feeling and sibling rivalry. And Jacob's choice of lentils may be dictated by a desire to find a vegetable equivalent for the heartiness and redness of meat.

The early rabbis, in the Midrash Genesis Rabba, have another explanation for the specification of lentils: it is a food served to mourners, and Jacob is mourning the death of his grandfather Abraham, a loss that Esau treats cavalierly. Needless to say, there is no hint of this circumstance of recent bereavement in the biblical account. But whenever we read, we make use of not only our predisposition to metaphor, our awareness of co-texts, and our possible adherence to interpretive authority, but also of our knowledge of the real world. It is clear that in the rabbinical milieu of late antiquity, lentils must have been a customary dish prepared for mourners. It is even possible that the practice goes back to the biblical period as well, though there is no specific evidence for it in the material that has come down to us, and the rabbinical habit of retrojection into the earlier era may lead the interpretation astray. This midrashic reading of the lentil stew, though it introduces a rather fanciful element of plot unstated in Genesis, is not figurative but mimetic. As readers, we always to some degree draw inferences about the function of a detail by referring it to what we know of its role in the social and historical realm beyond literature. If we imagined that all the rural bridges in Central Europe were made out of metal or stone, we might want to see in Kafka's wooden bridge a metaphor of the organic world, an emblem of the Tree of Knowledge, or any far-fetched figurative thing. As it is, we recognize commonsensically that Kafka is doing a bit of realistic scene setting. The detail may have no further significance, or it may be linked causally or analogically with other details as we follow what happens in the scene.

It should be apparent that my argument is edging back toward the literal. I would contend that there is no real contradiction between literal and figurative readings of narrative. On the contrary, the tendency of figurative readings to proliferate, even in cases like the one we have been considering in which the text itself seems to propose a univocal interpretation of the specified detail, points to a need always to return to the literal narrative data that give rise to the figurative readings. Jacob's lentil stew means Edom the Red—so the narrator plainly tells us. Perhaps it also suggests bloody Edom. Perhaps it is implicated in a whole domestic drama of love grotesquely traded for food, wounded filial emotions, fraternal jealousy, a sedentary way of life opposed to that of the hunter. The matrix of all these possibilities is a concrete entity in the world of the story. In the first instance, and the last, the lentil stew is a medium of exchange and a physical nexus between the brothers in this crucial episode—the presumably pungent, bubbling, and definitely dark red stuff in Jacob's pot. Whatever else we read into it, this stubborn materiality is not compromised.

Let me offer a simpler example in which the meaning of a narrative specification is clearly stated in the text. In this instance, the obtrusive materiality of the detail is quite horrific. In the first chapter of Judges, in an account of a Judahite campaign of conquest against the Canaanites, a Canaanite king named Adonibezek is captured and has his thumbs and big toes chopped off by his captors. Lest we wonder why this grisly detail need be conveyed, Adonibezek himself supplies an explanation: "Seventy kings with thumbs and big toes cut off would gather scraps under my table. As I have done, so has God paid me back" (Judg. 1:7). Thus, the maiming of Adonibezek is the carrying out of a stark principle of historical retribution. This Canaanite king has only a momentary role in the biblical chronicle, and so the detail of his maiming can hardly have the ramifications of Jacob's stew, standing as it does at the triangular conjunction of father and two brothers, all important characters. Nevertheless, the declared law of retribution, like the etiology of Edom in Genesis 25, refuses to stand still. In part this is because in the eyes of the biblical writers retribution is a more dialectic and a messier affair than one might imagine. Chapter 1 of Judges is, among other things, a kind of thematic prologue to the book as a whole. A salient image of chopping off body parts provides an entirely appropriate gateway into the world of Judges, with its long chain of murders and assassinations, bellies pierced with concealed daggers, foreheads shattered with tent pegs, bodies crushed by millstones, and, in a grand finale, the body of a gang-raped woman hacked into twelve pieces, which are sent to the sundry tribes in order to muster them to a devastating civil war against the tribe of Benjamin. Adonibezek, then, is telling us a good deal not only about his own bloody career but about the continuing history of Israel.

If, moreover, there is a still larger whole, in Frank Kermode's terms, to which this part is related, the ghastly fate of Adonibezek may also adumbrate the end of the whole First Commonwealth history in the last chapter of 2 Kings: the last Judean king, Zedekiah, has his eyes gouged out by his Babylonian captors as he is led off in chains, and his predecessor, Jehoiachin, is taken from his cell and granted a place at the table of the Babylonian king—a happier variant of the captive kings gathering scraps.[4] I am not in the least suggesting that Adonibezek is a typological preembodiment of Zedekiah or Jehoiachin. On the contrary, the hideous singularity of his fate stands out in the brief moment accorded it in the narrative sequence. The fact that those severed thumbs and toes generate meanings and possibilities of connection beyond what the character himself says about them brings us back to their insistent physicality. They may well be a manifestation of a *lex talionis*, as Adonibezek announces. They may also be a figure or thematic introduction for events and patterns of events that occur later. But they can be all this by presenting themselves to the reader's imagination as a horrendous literal fact, a datum of the *sensus historicus* in which a particular Canaanite king, famous for his savagery, was at a certain moment in the course of the conquest maimed in precisely this way by his captors.

Biblical narrative offers a second class of specification in which no meaning of the detail is spelled out but some thematic significance is strongly implicit. One of the most striking instances is the catalog of Goliath's armor and weapons at the beginning of 1 Samuel 17. The predominant biblical practice is not to say anything about what people are wearing and carrying unless it constitutes a necessary link in the plot, like Joseph's ornamented tunic. Goliath, however, is introduced with a kind of Homeric recitation of battle equipment— bronze helmet, mail armor, bronze greaves and javelin, iron-tipped spear, and shield, with fabulous weights stipulated for most of the items on the list. We do not have to read much further to see why all this is here. When the young David volunteers to fight Goliath, Saul fits him out with his own armor and helmet and sword. The shepherd boy, however, stumbles under the unaccustomed weight of all these accoutrements, puts them aside, and goes out to battle with his sling and five carefully chosen smooth stones. Just before he brings the Philistine giant crashing to the ground, he proclaims in his fighter's taunt to Goliath, "And all this assembly will know that neither by sword nor spear does the Lord grant victory, for the battle is the Lord's" (1 Sam. 17:47). The whole story, then, becomes a virtual allegory of this cardinal principle of biblical faith, the folkloric motif of the young hero slaying the ogre transformed into monotheistic theology. The catalog of Goliath's armor begins to look like an allegorical satire on displaced faith in the realm of quantified material implements.

This thematic impetus is reinforced by the intersection of the bigness of Goliath with the bigness of Saul. The first king of Israel is a hulking man, "head and shoulders taller" than any of his followers (1 Sam. 9:2). Pointedly, big Saul shows not the slightest inclination to be the champion who will confront huge Goliath. David is unable to fight in Saul's armor not only because he is unused to such equipment but because it is completely oversize for him. Yet his victory and the events of the subsequent narrative demonstrate that he is a better man for the throne than Saul. And bigness in relation to kingship is in fact explicitly thematized in the preceding chapter, in the episode of Samuel's clandestine anointment of David. Samuel is on the point of anointing Eliab, David's oldest brother, when God intervenes and warns him not to make the same mistake he made with Saul: "Look not at his appearance or his lofty stature, as I have rejected him. For it is not what man sees—man sees with his eyes and the Lord sees into the heart" (1 Sam. 16:7).

With all this, is there anything left of Goliath's great bulk and armor, or of Saul's unusual height, that is not a metaphor, symbol, or token of a theological theme? In the case of explicitly motivated narrative specification, the strong tendency of the detail to point toward meanings beyond the explicitly stated one had, we saw, the effect of bringing us back to the insistent presence in the narrative of the literal detail. The absence of explicit motivation has much the same effect because it compels inference, and there is always a margin of indeterminacy in inference. We have been aware of Saul's exceptional stature for seven eventful chapters before the Lord spells out the thematic principle at stake in his dialogue with Samuel. This is time enough for a reader to associate Saul's height with kingliness (a mistake, but perhaps not entirely a mistake), with his isolation, with a kind of heroic ungainliness or ineptitude. It becomes, in short, a synecdoche for Saul's distinctive identity and fate, a multifaceted thematic elaboration of the *sensus historicus,* for we may assume that the writer had good reason to believe, or at any rate believed in good faith, that the historical Saul was a very tall man.

Goliath, a minor and much simpler character, is a much simpler case. If one follows a method of reading the Bible recently proposed by the Israeli critic Harold Fisch,[5] one could say that a pagan tradition of epic poetry is invoked in the catalog of Goliath's armor only to be subverted. This is a reasonable enough explanation, but I would add an observation inspired by Mikhail Bakhtin—that when the discourse of another is incorporated in a literary text, even to be debated or invalidated, it is given, at least momentarily, a voice of its own. Goliath in his many hundredweights of bronze may be already implicitly a satiric target for the monotheistic writer, but he is also, in his moment as insulting alien challenger, a splendid, looming, scary figure, epic being allowed a fleeting appearance in the world of biblical narrative. Were it not so, David's triumph would be far less satisfying. Oral tradition and folklore offer countless stories of a giant or an ogre struck down by a young, hitherto unknown champion: but the specific literary articulation of this particular version has provided imaginative excitement to readers through the ages on two quite distinct levels. It has in fact been read as a kind of allegory, for the reasons we have seen, with the very phrase

"David and Goliath" turned into proverbial shorthand for the triumph of the seemingly weak over the strong. It has also, through the specificity of its artful articulation, invited readers to enjoy it for what it literally is, to imagine the huge figure of Goliath in all his armor, terrificly his bulking, martial self, clanking toward the field of battle, where he is awaited by a poised adolescent carrying five smooth stones in a leather pouch.

I have reserved for the end the category of narrative specification that might present the strongest evidence for the persistence of the literal—the seemingly extraneous detail for which no explanation is offered and for which the surrounding narrative provides no obvious thematic clues. In these instances, too, one can glimpse signs of that coexistence of the literal and the figurative for which I have been arguing, though the possibilities of the figurative will be more open-ended and speculative, constituting a kind of semantic penumbra around the concreteness of the literal object, as in the case of Flaubert's barometer. Let me offer one piquant example that is fairly characteristic of biblical narrative practice.

In the early chapters of 1 Samuel, the ark of the Lord, having been imprudently carried out to the battlefield by the Israelites, is captured by the Philistines and then wreaks havoc among its captors in the form of plagues and the destruction of Philistine cultic objects. The Philistines, realizing they have latched onto dangerous material, ask their priests what should be done, and the priests prescribe a kind of oracular trial by ordeal. The ark, together with an offering of gold icons, is to be placed on a new cart drawn by two milch cows that have never before borne a yoke, while their calves are to be penned up so that they cannot follow their mothers. If the milch cows pull the cart on the road to Israelite Beth-Shemesh, the Philistines will know that all their woes have been caused by the Israelite God and must allow the ark

to be returned to its original possessors with the golden trib-
ute. What happens is conveyed in the following terms: "And
the cows went straight on the road, on the road to Beth-
Shemesh, on a single highroad, lowing as they went, veering
neither right nor left" (1 Sam. 6:12).

There is emphatic synonymity in this report ("on the road,"
"the road to Beth-Shemesh," "on a single highroad," "went
straight," "veering neither right nor left"), which obviously
serves to underline that the stipulation of the Philistine priests
is fulfilled without the slightest doubt or possibility of devia-
tion: the arrow-straight trajectory thus demonstrates to the
Philistines that the hand of the Lord has wrought all these
things. But what is the need for the detail of the cows lowing?
By the rigorously economical standards of biblical narrative, it
is an extraneous specification almost startling in its concreteness that serves no purpose of plot and no evident purpose of
theme. As I have been insisting all along, the primary fact
about the detail is its force of literal presence in the world of
narrated events. If I can presume to reconstruct what is
behind the narrative specification from the viewpoint of the
Hebrew writer, it might be something like this: The general
purpose of the story is pointedly ideological. At this juncture
of the narrative, a test proposed by the Philistine priests themselves will be used to prove once again the overriding power
of the Lord of Israel against the impotence of the nonentity
gods of the pagans. The abundant synonymous language for
the straight course of the milch cows stems from a stylistic
choice that makes clear the theological point to be demonstrated. But even in the midst of such an urgently purposeful
narrative, the writer is not immune to the attraction of mimesis for its own gratifying sake. What a nice little touch, he
must have felt even if he would not consciously have put it in
those terms, to catch the vividness of the moment by includ-

ing the lowing of the cows as they make their ordained way to Beth-Shemesh.

Even in such an instance, however, meaning resists being limited conclusively to the literal. This resistance is the result of a collusion between the first and the second of Frank Kermode's three reasons for the elusiveness of the plain sense—the habit of metaphor and the gravitational pull of co-texts. That is, as we read, we constantly grasp, whether consciously or not, for analogies to what we have already read, and writers at all times and places exhibit a tendency to structure narrative as a complex system of analogies of differing scale, from correspondences of incident to recurrent images and phrases or even syntactical patterns. (In another connection, I have characterized this tendency as the "mnemonic force" of the literary text.)[6] As a general rule, analogy plays a more important role in biblical narrative than in most other kinds of narrative because the art of the ancient Hebrew tale usually avoids explicit commentary by the narrator and instead invites us to see connections and even evaluative perspectives through an awareness or intuition of correspondences between one part of the story and another.

Our poor milch cows—on their unwitting way to be consumed as burnt offerings to the Lord—are lowing because their udders are full of milk for the calves they have left behind them penned up in the Philistine town of Ekron. This manifest violation of animal rights is presumably necessary in order to demonstrate that the Lord can work his will against the grain of nature, causing the cows to head on a straight path away from their calves to Israelite Beth-Shemesh. But the lowing of the cows rhymes weirdly, and suggestively, with the story of the birth of Samuel that immediately precedes it and that serves as the great prelude to the account of the painful founding of the monarchy in 1 and 2 Samuel. Hannah,

one recalls, the future mother of Samuel, is barren and tear-
fully prays to the Lord at the Shiloh sanctuary to grant her the
blessing of male offspring. After the prayer is answered, having pledged the son to the Lord, she keeps the child with her
"and gave suck to her son until she weaned him" (1 Sam.
1:23). Only then, and one may guess it was a protracted nurs-
ing period (he is already a *na'ar*, a "lad"), does she bring him
to the sanctuary and entrust him to the care of Eli the priest.
The biblical narrator, adhering to his general norm of impas-
sivity, tells us nothing directly of Hannah's feelings in this
freely accepted separation from her precious firstborn son, but
he beautifully intimates her devotion to the child she has sur-
rendered in a small detail reported in the next chapter: "And
his mother would make him a little robe and she would bring
it up to him each year when she and her husband came to sacrifice the annual sacrifice" (1 Sam. 2:19).

There is no way of knowing whether the writer actually
calculated a correspondence between these two episodes, and
I don't think it is important to decide the issue of conscious
intention. The literary text exercises mnemonic force to a large
extent because all sorts of links and parallels are activated in
the process of literary imagination of which the writer, knowing more than he realizes, is not necessarily aware. The Book
of Samuel begins with the poignant story of an anguished barren woman who is at last vouchsafed a son, must devote him
to the Lord's sanctuary once he is weaned, and afterward sees
him only at the time of the annual sacrifice, when she brings
him a token of her love. The story of the return of the ark
offers a parallel and complementary image of the two lowing
cows, separated from their still unweaned offspring, on the
way to being sacrificed to the Lord. The milch cows are by no
means a symbol or allegory of something else, but the
dynamic of mutual reinforcement created by the correspon-

dences between the episodes sets up a kind of thematic force field at the beginning of the Book of Samuel.

Divine election is an exacting and perhaps cruel destiny that often involves doing violence to the most intimate biological bonds. When Saul sets out to look for the lost asses, he begins to worry that his father may become anxious about his protracted absence from home. Once Saul is chosen king, his parents disappear from the picture, only a somewhat enigmatic uncle making a brief appearance. David's Bethlehem family of origin similarly vanishes, or is abandoned, once he begins to pursue his career to the throne. Saul's son Jonathan and his daughter Michal then implicitly reject him by placing first their loyalty and affection for David, the man who becomes the Lord's new choice as anointed one. David in turn nearly loses the throne to one of his own sons, and his offspring produce a miasma of fratricide, scheming, and maneuvering against each other and against their father that clouds his latter years. If the Hebrew writers conceive Israelite history as the play of power in the always uncertain effort to carry out God's aims in the arena of political events, there is a strong sense in these stories that human submission to these aims exacts a terrible price, tearing through the ligatures that bind parent and child, displacing people from the organic realm of biological connection to the sometimes murderous and usually corrupting realm of politics.

I am not claiming that all this is clearly represented in the lowing milch cows but only that the gratuitous detail also has an indeterminate thematic functionality. The rule of thumb is that the open-ended semantic nature of the detail, its power to intimate shifting clusters of figurative meanings, is a direct consequence of its literal force in the narrated world. The case of unmotivated narrative specification exemplifies this productive dialectic tension between literal and figurative.

Various possibilities for reading the episode in question and the larger story may open up if we begin to see analogies between udder and breast, between an improvised stone altar outside Beth-Shemesh and the sanctuary at Shiloh. What remains, however, always in the foreground of the reading experience is the visual and auditory image of two milch cows lowing as they haul a cart on an unswerving course to Israelite territory, leaving their calves forever behind them.

Biblical narrative, because it is sparing in detail and abstemious about narratorial intervention, offers some of the most splendid illustrations in the Western literary tradition of the power of strategically introduced specification. It has been endlessly subjected to allegorical, tropological, anagogical, and all sorts of other readings beyond the famous four levels of interpretation invoked by Dante as by the rabbis. It has been able to sustain all these readings not merely because of the expectations of divinely revealed truth that Jewish and Christian readers brought to it but also because of the arresting, never exhaustively motivated presence of its literal details. The life of narrative inheres in the potency of the literal, and also, paradoxically, it is the literal that creates the potential of narrative to mean many things.

CHAPTER 5

Allusion and Literary Expression

Nothing confirms the literary character of biblical narrative and biblical poetry more strikingly than their constant, resourceful, and necessary recourse to allusion. Now, it is obvious that, because the members of any culture carry around in their heads bits and pieces of all sorts of texts, allusion also occurs quite abundantly in nonliterary discourse, both written and spoken. A newspaper article, say, about the collapse of an African government may invoke T. S. Eliot's "not with a bang but a whimper," or a phrase from Lincoln's Gettysburg Address, or a line from *Hamlet*, or a prescription from *Robert's Rules of Order*. On the whole, such allusions to familiar texts in ordinary speech, journalism, and most expository writing work as rhetorical embellishments; there is rarely a sense that they are dictated by the necessity of the form of expression in which they occur.

The case is quite different with literature. A person inevitably composes a story or poem—and it makes no difference whether the composition is written or oral—out of the awareness of a preexisting body of textual objects, stories or poems, in which the composition at hand will constitute a new member. Thus, every writer not only emulates certain models but is compelled to define a relationship—competitive, admiring, revisionist, elaborative—to at least certain elements of antecedent literary tradition. Allusion, then, is not an embellishment but a fundamental necessity of literary expression: the writer, scarcely able to ignore the texts that have anticipated him and in some sense given him the very idea of writing, appropriates fragments of them, qualifies or transforms them, uses them to give his own work both a genealogy and a resonant background.

The Russian semiotician Jurij Lotman has characterized literature as a "secondary language" whose code of communication is manifested in the complex set of conventions, generic norms, images, and actual texts shared by different writers. Building on this perception, the French literary theorist Laurent Jenny argues that, "without intertextuality, a literary work would simply be unintelligible, like speech in a language one has not yet learned." He goes on to speak of the *archetypes* of literary discourse, a term that does not, I think, sufficiently suggest the kinds of highly specific, textually microscopic allusions that often occur in literary texts. In any case, he is surely right in his notion that the meanings of any work of literature are enacted through a fulfillment or revision of inherited materials: "The literary work's relation to these archetypal models is always one of realization, transformation, or transgression."[1]

It is just such a process of realization, transformation, and transgression of antecedent biblical texts—not to speak of texts in other ancient Near Eastern literatures—that is constantly observable in the Bible. If *transgression* seems too strong a term, we might recall the great death-wish poem of Job 3—an extreme case but by no means a unique one—which reverses the terms of creation at the beginning of Genesis with terrific imaginative power. Poetry may have a generic predisposition to remember literary antecedents in a more minutely textual way than prose usually does, but I would like to show how the same dynamic of allusion repeatedly operates in biblical prose. Against the tendency to isolate and analyze, I want to argue for our obligation as readers to put together the disparate pieces of biblical narrative.

Putting together biblical narrative suggests that someone has taken it apart, and that has indeed been the principal occupation of formidable intellectual energies in the academic study of the Bible for over a century and a half. Let me hasten to say that if we murder to dissect, we also dissect to understand, and nothing in what follows is meant to discount the impressive advances in the understanding of the historical development of the Bible that have been achieved through the analysis of its text, whatever the margin of conjecture, into disparate components. But unfortunately, scholarly attention, like other forms of human attention, has difficulty in focusing on more than one order of objects at a time, and the concentration on dissected elements has led to a relative neglect of the complex means used by the biblical writers to lock their texts together, to amplify their meanings by linking one text with another. If biblical scholarship has been guided by a tacit imperative that might be formulated, as I observed earlier, (see page 70) as *the more atomistic, the more scientific,* it also needs to be recognized that the atoms were often purposefully assembled by the writers into intricate, integrated structures, which are, after all, what we experience as readers and which abundantly deserve scholarly consideration.

It should be noted that increasing attention—in part

inspired by the new literary analysis of the Bible—has in recent years been devoted to the ways in which biblical texts meaningfully refer to other biblical texts, and one enterprising new study, David Damrosch's *The Narrative Covenant*,[2] boldly attempts to identify such interconnections while at the same time building on the discrimination of historically distinct textual layers proposed by analytic scholarship. In any case, the biblical writer's use of allusion as a conscious literary device deserves to be studied with some care, for in both its range of formal deployments and its variety of modes of signification it reveals much of the artful complication of ancient Hebrew narrative.

Allusion to antecedent literary texts is an indispensable mechanism of all literature, virtually dictated by the self-recapitulative logic of literary expression. No one writes a poem or a story without some awareness of other poems or stories to emulate, pay homage to, vie with, criticize, or parody, and so the evocation of phrases, images, motifs, situations from antecedent texts is an essential part of the business of making new texts. For reasons that I hope will soon be clearer, the corpus of ancient Hebrew literature that has come down to us in the Bible exhibits a remarkable density of such allusions. Now, some may object that the sort of dynamic that comes into play when, say, T. S. Eliot alludes to Shakespeare and Milton cannot be applied to the Bible, which represents a "scribal culture" that makes frequent use not of literary allusion but of traditional formulas, verbal stereotypes. The whole notion of formula, so often invoked in biblical scholarship, needs serious critical reexamination because there is such an abundance of subtle, significant *variations* in the biblical use of formulas, but that is an undertaking that lies beyond our present purpose. In any case, the Bible offers rich and varied evidence of the most purposeful literary allusions—not the recurrence of fixed formula or conventional stereotype but a pointed activation of one text by another,[3] conveying a connection in difference or a difference in connection through some conspicuous similarity in phrasing, in motif, or in narrative situation.

The marker for the allusion may be as economical as a single unusual or strategically placed word or as profuse as a whole episode parallel in situation to and abounding in citations from an earlier episode. The infant Moses is placed in an "ark" (*tevah*) and set among the bulrushes, to be saved from the decree of drowning that Pharaoh has issued for all Hebrew male babies (Exod. 2:3). The solitary term *tevah* recalls the ark in which Noah and his family and the specimens of the sundry species were saved from the universal drowning that engulfed all living things, and the Noah story, which itself involved a renewal of the first creation, leads back in turn to a cluster of reminiscences of Genesis 1 in Exodus 1.[4] Thus, the Exodus story is marked as a new beginning, a resumption of the process of God-given creation and procreation derailed by an oppressor. At the other end of the spectrum of allusive markers, the horrendous tale of the concubine at Gibeah in Judges 19 is an elaborate replay of the story of the two angels' visit to Lot's house in Sodom in Genesis 19 (the identity of chapter numbers, which are the product of medieval editorial conventions, is of course mere coincidence). In both, two strangers are taken in by the only hospitable household in town; in both, the brutish populace wants to gang-rape the male guest, or guests; in both, the host offers the mob two women instead; and the author of Judges 19 quotes sentence after sentence of dialogue and narratorial report from Genesis 19, making only minor changes in the language.

The relation of the concubine in Gibeah to the Sodom story raises two methodological issues that may help clarify the place of allusion in biblical narrative. The first is the question of dating that has been an endless source of perplexity in biblical studies. Allusion, of course, presupposes the temporal priority of one text to another. To contemplate for a moment an extreme possibility, do we know that Judges was written later than Genesis, or that its author was really familiar with Genesis? Might Genesis even be alluding to Judges, and not the other way around? Such a hypothesis is extremely unlikely first because the language of the story in Judges gives evidence of being an *elaboration* of the language in Genesis 19, going beyond the classical terseness of the Sodom narrative through the addition of little phrases that make the moral judgment of the events more explicit. If, moreover, there were no actual allusion to Sodom in Gibeah, the whole conspicuous function of Sodom as moral paradigm would be lost. In biblical literature, Sodom, not Gibeah, is the proverbial model of a wholly depraved society that condemns itself to destruction; the Hebrew writers repeatedly want to trouble Israel with the grim possibility that it may turn into Sodom, its supposed antitype.[5]

This notion of paradigm undermines a second hypothesis that might be entertained as an alternative to allusion—that Genesis 19 and Judges 19 represent two different versions (the only ones that have survived) of a conventional, stereotypical tale about the violation of hospitality that circulated in the folklore of ancient Israel. In fact, none of the biblical episodes strikingly similar to each other in plot and theme—what elsewhere I have called type-scenes—exhibits the kind of extensive sharing of actual language that we find in these two texts. The only plausible inference is that the author of Judges 19 had a minute textual familiarity with Genesis in a version that must have been fairly close to the one that has come down to us—and analogous evidence in the use of allusion can be cited to indicate that the authors of the Former Prophets in general were familiar with much of the received version of the

Tetrateuch. The writer in Judges, addressing himself to the origins of a murderous civil war, wanted to show his audience what could happen when an Israelite community casts away the fundamental bonds of civilized intercourse. This moral possibility was etched in fire and brimstone in the story of Sodom, from which he felt free to quote extensively, while firmly stressing that, in the nonmiraculous, political framework of his own story, there are no angels to intervene, the wayfaring Levite behaves like anything but an angel, a woman is raped to death, and the agency of retribution is not divine fire but bloody civil strife.

Allusion is pervasive in the Bible, to begin with, for the mechanical reason I have just cited—that this was, on the evidence of the texts themselves, a traditional culture that encouraged a high degree of verbatim retention of its own classical texts. A local indication of the assumption of retentiveness is the constant use of the technique of near-verbatim repetition of clauses and sentences within a single episode. Again and again, a revelation of a shift in attitude, perspective, or situation is introduced through the alteration of a single word, the deletion of a phrase, the addition of a word, a switch in the order of items, as statements are repeated; it is a technique with a power and subtlety that could have worked only on an audience accustomed to retain minute textual details as it listened and thus to recognize the small but crucial changes introduced in repetition. A listener who could in this way detect close recurrence and difference within the frame of a single episode might reasonably have been expected to pick up a good many verbal echoes and situational correspondences between far-flung episodes. As I shall try to show, the biblical conception of history and the common biblical ideology often provided compelling reasons for the use of allusion in the Bible, but there is also a good deal of allusion in the Bible, as in other literatures, that is more local in intention: a given story evokes some moment in an antecedent story strictly for the narrative purposes at hand, to underline a theme, define a motive or character, provide a certain orientation toward an event.

In 2 Samuel 13, David's son Amnon, preparatory to raping his half sister Tamar, gives the order "Take everyone out from before me" (verse 9), the identical words—*hotsi'u khol 'ish me`alai*—that Joseph uses (Gen. 45:1) when he wants to clear the viceregal chamber before he tells his brothers that he is Joseph. The momentary irony is clear and pointed: the same words that were a preface to a great moment of fraternal reconciliation are now a prologue to a sexual violation of the fraternal bond. But the connections between Amnon and Joseph reach more to the heart of Amnon's story, the ironic dissonances sharpening as the terrible tale progresses. Once brother and sister are alone in his bedroom, Amnon, who has been pretending illness, seizes Tamar, making only the most terse and unadorned statement (in the Hebrew, just four words) of his lust, "Come lie with me, my sister." This brutally direct imperative echoes the two-word (Hebrew) speech in Genesis 39, which is all that Potiphar's wife is reported to have said to Joseph: "Lie with me."

Interestingly—indeed, almost teasingly—the allusion to Genesis 39 is not only verbal but also structural. In the Joseph story, that is, the high moral satire of the concupiscent Egyptian lady is pointed up by a structure of contrastive dialogue in which she has only two words as the language of her desire, while he is full of nervous volubility in reminding her of his status, his responsibilities toward his master, and the iniquity of consummating such an act of betrayal. In the story of Amnon and Tamar, the assailant is again laconic in lust (and after the rape, he has just two words for her, *qumi lekhi,* "get out"), while the assailed one, Tamar, speaks eight words for every one of his—as she desperately tries to ward him off by reminding him of the baseness of the act and the shame that will attach to her, raising the possibility that he can have her legally if he asks it of the king, their father. The links with Joseph are then made explicit in an odd detail of royal sartorial custom that the writer appends to the rape narrative. After Amnon has his servants thrust Tamar out, referring to her contemptuously as *zot*, "this one" (with the force of "this creature"), and bolting the door behind her, we are told that "she had on a coat of many colors [*ketonet pasim*], for such were the robes that the virgin daughters of the king would wear" (verse 18). Joseph, of course, is conspicuously associated with a coat of many colors—is, in fact, the only other figure in the Hebrew Bible said to wear such a garment.

This confluence of allusions to the Joseph story gives thematic depth to the tale of incestuous rape. The episode begins with an echo of Joseph's reconciliation scene and moves back in reverse narrative direction to the ornamental tunic, which in the Joseph story marks the initial crime of brothers against brother, when they attacked him and fabricated out of the blood-soaked garment the evidence of his death. Tamar, at the end a victim of fraternal hatred, like Joseph at the beginning, tears her tunic as a sign of mourning, and her fine garment, like his, may well be bloodstained, if one considers that she has just lost her virginity by rape. (Allusion being a two-way street, the detail of royal costume here may also throw backward light on the Joseph story, suggesting that Jacob's extravagant and provocative gift of the coat of many colors could be a gesture of conferring quasi-regal status on his decidedly virginal son.)

The strife among brothers of the Joseph story is pertinent not only to this episode but to its ramified consequences. Absalom, Tamar's full brother, vows vengeance, and after the passage of two years he has his henchmen murder Amnon. This act leads to his banishment from David's court and, eventually, to his rebellion against David. The entire second half of the David story is an account of the aging king's loss of control over his wayward sons, and the allusion to Joseph in this episode, which is the very moment when things begin to fall apart, may indicate a general parallel to the aging Jacob, who from the time of the massacre of the male population of Shechem (another act of vengeance in response to a sister's being raped) is repeatedly at the mercy of his intransigent sons.

The rape itself represents a pointed reversal of the scene between Joseph and Potiphar's wife. At least in this sexual arena, anatomy does prove to be destiny. When the importunate lady's two words of sexual command are unavailing, she initiates what looks like an attempt at rape, "seizing" Joseph as Amnon will take hold of his sister. But the young man, too quick and too strong for the woman, is able to wrench away from her and flee, leaving his garment (still another piece of clothing to be adduced as false evidence) in her hand. When, however, it is the man who is the assailant, the woman is, quite literally, overpowered, a point the narrator takes pains to bring home to us in a string of three verbs where one would suffice, "he was stronger than she, and ravished her, and lay with her" (verse 14). The evocation of Genesis 39 with the sexual roles reversed might even reflect one of those flickerings of feminist consciousness one finds in the patriarchal Bible: Tamar's vulnerability as a woman is equally stressed in her powerlessness vis-à-vis the rapist and in the social disgrace consequent upon the violation.

In any event, Joseph's successful resistance to the sexual assault, though it leads to his imprisonment, is a way station in his spectacular ascent to royal power, whereas the victimization of Tamar triggers a process of internecine havoc in the royal house of David that will continue till the king is on his deathbed. The story of Amnon and Tamar has its own coherence and thus may easily be read without reference to the Joseph story, but to do so would be to rob it of some of its deepest thematic resonances, to fail to see the full implications of the particular episode, of the collision of character and gender, and of the larger political plot. Here, as almost everywhere in literature, the writer has shaped his meanings by aligning his text with memorable moments in the inherited literary tradition that are at once parallel and antithetical to his own narrative materials.[6]

In the Bible, however, the matrix for allusion is often a sense of absolute historical continuity and recurrence, or an assumption that earlier events and figures are timeless ideological models by which all that follows can be measured. Since many of the biblical writers saw history as a pattern of cyclical repetition of events, there are abundant instances of this first category of allusion, none more striking than the beginning of the Book of Joshua. These chapters pick up the thread of narrative that has been interrupted by Moses' long valedictory address, which constitutes the whole of Deuteronomy. In a large-scale deployment of what biblical scholars call resumptive repetition—that is, after an interpolation, the last phrases before the narrative broke off are repeated—the beginning of Joshua takes us back in a variety of ways to the early chapters of Exodus. The warrant for these allusions is not merely formal but also conceptual because the conquest of the land that Joshua is about to launch after the death of Moses is seen as a second Exodus, a significant new stage in the process of national liberation begun in the emancipation from Egyptian bondage.

The first object of conquest, as everyone recalls, is the city of Jericho, just to the west of the Jordan River, and the miraculous collapse of its walls is reported in Chapter 6. It may be that the miracle itself, through the blasting of rams' horns and shouting preceded by seven days of complete silence enjoined

on the Israelites, harks back to Moses' words to Israel at the
Sea of Reeds, "The Lord will fight for you and you will be
silent" (Exod. 14:14). But I would like to concentrate on the
allusive deployment of the five chapters that precede this
spectacular event. The first chapter is taken up with God's
pledge to give the Israelites the land, his injunction that they
depart not from his teaching, and the Israelites' answering
pledge to listen and perform all that God requires of them.
The chapter, full of Deuteronomic phrasing, is structurally apt
as a resumption of the themes of Moses' valedictory address
just concluded, and it need not detain us further here. Chapter
2 is the story of the two spies sent to Jericho. Chapter 3 reports
the crossing of the Jordan by the assembled tribes of Israel,
and Chapter 4 the memorialization of this event by the setting
up of twelve stone markers. Chapter 5 is an account of the
mass circumcision performed at Gilgal after the forty years in
the Wilderness, during which circumcision was not practiced,
a ritual here carried out as an act of national dedication
enabling the people to partake of the paschal sacrifice immediately preparatory to the beginning of the war of conquest.
We may be able to see the strong links with Exodus better by
beginning with this last episode and working backward.

    After the mass circumcision and the celebration of the
paschal feast (which is itself a ritual reenactment of the last
night in Egypt before the Exodus), Joshua, standing alone outside Jericho, encounters a "man" who confronts him sword in
hand. "Friend or foe?" Joshua challenges the stranger, who
responds by proclaiming himself "captain of the Lord's host."
Joshua at once prostrates himself, and then, perhaps surprisingly, the divine officer delivers neither prophecy nor exhortation but only the following words: "Take your shoes off
your feet, for the place you stand upon is holy" (Josh. 5:15).
The explicit verbal echoes from the Moses story are unmistak-
able, their most obvious function being to represent Joshua as

a second Moses. The structural correspondences, however, between the two stories are complicated, pointing to differences as well as to connections between the two figures. The whole chapter, which is essentially Joshua's dedication after that of Israel, is a replay of early episodes in the Moses story in reverse order, almost as if a film reel of the events from Exodus had been run backward. The shepherd Moses encounters God in the burning bush at Mount Horeb and is instructed, "Take your shoes off your feet, for the place you stand upon is holy ground" (Exod. 3:5). The sequence of action is as follows: the epiphany of the burning bush; Moses' reluctant acceptance of his mission; the tremendously compact and enigmatic encounter (Exod. 4:24–26) with the threatening figure of the Lord "on the way, at the encampment"; the act of circumcision that wards off the threat of death; the beginning of Moses' arduous task in Egypt. In the Joshua story, the sequence is first circumcision, then the appearance of the sword-wielding divine figure, which then turns into a benign epiphany echoing the Mount Horeb experience, and finally, as in the Moses story, the beginning of the hero's mission.

Smaller verbal clues, in addition to the actual quotation of Exodus 3:5 in the angel's words, link the two stories. The mass circumcision is performed with flint knives, just as Zipporah seized a flint to circumcise her son and avert the threat of death in Exodus 4. Explaining the need for the circumcision at Gilgal, the narrator observes that "they did not circumcise them *on the way*" (Josh. 5:5)—*baderekh*, as at the beginning of the Bridegroom of Blood story in Exodus 4 ("And it came to pass on the way, at the encampment . . ."). The condition of being uncircumcised is instructively called "the shame [KJV, "reproach"] of Egypt," a slightly odd designation, considering the information we are given here that the Israelites who came out of Egypt were circumcised, whereas the generation born in the Wilderness was not. (Whether the writer knew that circumcision was practiced among the Egyptians themselves is unclear.) The point is to associate the lack of circumcision with the pagan realm in which the people were enslaved and to mark the circumcision as a step in the process of liberation—which means, taking on a covenantal national identity—that was initiated in the flight from Egypt.

Let me now briefly sort out this whole set of correspondences in the interest of seeing what a nice instrument of expression allusion can be in the hands of the biblical writer. In the Moses story, the point of departure is the theophany, as Moses, "the master of all prophets," is later the chief recipient of Israel's greatest theophany. The encounter with the Lord at the encampment involves an actual threat of death, perhaps in keeping with Moses' own impulsive killing of the Egyptian taskmaster and certainly in adumbration of the Lord's slaying of all the firstborn of Egypt. The circumcision, which has a magical or apotropaic effect, must be dictated by a violent reminder from the divinity because Moses has married and begotten his son in alien Midian, and now has to reenter the covenantal frame of Israel as he assumes his task of leadership. By contrast, Joshua is a second Moses, not the first, a leader who is also a follower, not a founder. The covenantal framework is already standing; it is strongly invoked in Chapter 1, and in Chapter 5 God can appropriately begin with a general command to renew the ritual of circumcision, which the people carry out as a matter of course. After this dedication in the flesh comes the appearance of the divine stranger, who at first seems threatening but in fact is not. To Joshua the military man, what is revealed is not God himself or any pyrotechnic miracle, but the commander in chief of God's forces, and Joshua's initial challenge to him is that of a good sentinel, "Friend or foe?"

The theophany itself is muted, for Joshua's role is not really that of a prophet: the fact of revelation is chiefly a confirmation of the process of dedication before the beginning of the conquest. When the Lord tells Moses he is standing on holy ground, it is because there the Lord is present to him and also because on that mountain the Lord will reveal himself again, amid thunder and lightning, to give Israel his commandments. When the captain of the Lord's host tells Joshua he is standing on holy ground, that is in part because it is the place of revelation but also because it is the soil of the Promised Land that Israel through Joshua's leadership is enjoined to possess.

If we now move backward in the expository sequence at the beginning of Joshua, Chapters 3 and 4 are set out as a reenactment of the miraculous crossing of the Sea of Reeds in Exodus 14 and the memorialization of that event in the Song of the Sea, Exodus 15. The allusions of Chapter 3, in which the priests cross the Jordan dry-shod while the water stands in a heap (*ned*), as at the Sea of Reeds, are perfectly explicit: the episode is a preeminent illustration of the biblical notion that historical events exhibit patterned repetition, in a sense dramatically recur as a manifestation of providential design. The link between Joshua 4 and Exodus 15 is more structural correspondence than explicit allusion: in the play of primal national energies of the Exodus narrative, the miraculous event is commemorated by the rhapsodic celebratory gesture of song, accompanied by timbrels and dancing; in this later phase, the commemoration is ritualized in the erection of stone markers that reflect the formal division of the tribes and are associated with a miracle vouchsafed not the whole people but rather its priestly caste alone.

The most ingenious allusion to Exodus in these initial episodes occurs in the story of the two spies in Chapter 2. Now, there is a more obvious allusion here to the twelve spies in Numbers 13, a connection Jewish tradition rightly per-

ceived when it chose Joshua 2 as the portion from the
Prophets to be read in synagogue along with the Torah reading that includes Numbers 13. In Numbers there are two reso-
lute spies (Joshua and Caleb) and ten cowardly ones. Here
there are only two dependable spies who in a sense make
restitution for the collective failure of their predecessors. But
the restitution, it should be stressed, is represented as a
resumption of the process of the Exodus interrupted for forty
years by the fearful report of the spies who were sent out by
Moses.

When the king of Jericho gets word that strangers have
sneaked into the city, he asks Rahab the harlot, who has taken
them in, where they are. She pretends they have already fled
and encourages the king to set out in pursuit of them. In fact,
she has hidden them in the thatched roof of her house on the
city wall. When she climbs up to tell them what has happened
and to give them instructions for a safe escape, she feels
impelled to explain why she is helping them. Her first words
are "I know that the Lord has given you the land, and that
your terror has fallen upon us, and that all the inhabitants of
the land faint before you" (Josh. 2:9). The second and third
clauses are a close paraphrase of the end of one line and the
beginning of another in the Song of the Sea, with the order of
the lines reversed and the tight verse rhythm loosened into
prose: "All the inhabitants of Canaan faint. / Terror and fear
fall upon them" (Exod. 15:14–15). The allusion to Exodus 15 is
then spelled out as Rahab immediately goes on to say, "For
we have heard how the Lord dried up the waters of the Sea of
Reeds before you when you came out of Egypt" (Josh. 2:10). If
she has heard the sensational news, as a Canaanite she presumably has not heard the actual words of Moses' song of triumph at the sea, though the two spies might well recognize
her unwitting citation of the poem, and the Israelite audience
of the story certainly would.

By means of the allusion, the truth of history speaks through the mouth of a Canaanite harlot. The Song of the Sea, which follows two stanzas on the victory over the Egyptian host with a third stanza anticipating a similar triumph over the peoples of Canaan, is seen to be literally predictive rather than poetically hyperbolic. As one of the inhabitants of the land herself bears witness, terror of the Israelites *has* fallen upon them; the Canaanites indeed faint before the Israelite host. The allusion in the dialogue assigned to Rahab announces the keynote for the reenactment of Exodus that will follow. She sends the spies off "to the mountain" to wait there three days, as Moses took the Israelites out of Egypt to the mountain where they would wait three days before the giving of the Law. The spies, in turn, give Rahab a sign to protect her household from the Israelite onslaught to come: she is to place a scarlet thread in her window, as in Exodus the Hebrews smeared blood over the doorposts to protect their houses from the deadly sweep of the tenth plague. Afterward, the whole sequence we have reviewed unfolds: the new crossing of waters, the new commemoration, the circumcision, the encounter with the armed angel that becomes a reassuring epiphany. In all this, the larger symmetry of the story is underscored: Israel passes across a threshold of water from bondage into the "liminal" sphere of the Wilderness, and then crosses a second threshold of water into the land, after undergoing appropriate experiences of dedication and revelation that recall the very first stages of its movement toward liberation forty years earlier.[7]

The kind of allusion we have been considering is a way of making two stories into one continuous story. Joshua, after all, is the immediate successor to Moses, and through the play of allusion he and his followers are seen to repeat, with significant differences, the acts of Moses and the preceding generation. But in the larger biblical panorama of narrative that spans eras of Israelite history, many stories cannot be contiguous in this way, and so allusion often involves not the continuity of reenactment but the evocation of a figure or an event in an earlier text that serves as a moral touchstone. A central concern, for example, of all biblical literature is the question of leadership. Ancient Israel makes no absolute distinction between civic and spiritual leadership, so this is at once a political and a religious question. A whole set of models for leaders faced with challenges, frequently in conflict with their followers, is offered by the Wilderness stories in Exodus and Numbers. Before these, many of the underlying political issues are adumbrated in the tales of rivalry, conflict, and resolution within the family in Genesis.

Among the later historical books, the one that is explicitly constructed as an exploration of the spectrum of possibilities of leadership—they progress from good to flawed to disastrous—is the Book of Judges. The background of the people's political predicaments in its formative period is invoked as early as Chapter 2, when a verse that is a prelude to the Exodus story is transposed into an element in the prelude to the history of the Judges: "And there arose another generation that knew not the Lord" (Judg. 2:10).[8] In Exodus 1:8, it is of course a new king who knew not Joseph. The disturbing reversal, in which language referring to an alien king's iniquitous relation to Israel is attached to Israel's relation to God, is characteristic of the often dissonant use of allusion in Judges. Whether one is talking about conjectured editors supposedly responsible for the Deuteronomistic framework or about the authors of the stories proper (and in my view scholarship has seriously overstated the difference between the two), the world of this book is one in which covenantal faith repeatedly collapses into pagan excess and social order into sheer mayhem. The echoes, then, of earlier Hebrew literature frequently point up the ways in which Israelite behavior has fallen precipitously from its founding models. Dissonant allusion is sometimes emphatically applied to the wayward populace, while the leaders, who are usually a mixture of strengths and flaws, are defined through a junction of consonant and dissonant allusions.

In Chapter 8, Gideon, who began his career as an idol smasher, successfully completes a campaign against the Midianite marauders who had terrorized Israel. Pursuing the enemy forces to their trans-Jordanian bases, he captures their chieftains Zebah and Zalmunnah, who admit to having murdered his kinsmen, and he kills them himself, then takes the crescent ornaments from the necks of their camels. His men respond to the victory as follows:

> And the men of Israel said to Gideon, "Rule over us, both you, and your son, and your son's son, for you have liberated us from the hand of Midian." And Gideon said to them, "I will not rule over you, and my son will not rule over you. The Lord will rule over you." And Gideon said to them, "Let me ask something of you: give me each of you the earring he has taken as booty." For they had gold earrings, as they were Ishmaelites. And they said, "We will certainly give." And they spread out the cloak and every man cast therein the earring he had taken as booty. (Judg. 8:22–25)

The intrusion of Ishmaelites into a story that all along has been about Midianites is a puzzlement. It is generally explained as one of those famous slippages of terminology and traditions that can be detected in the Bible. That is, a later period identified the nomadic martial and mercantile people of the trans-Jordan as Ishmaelites, and the writer or editor evidently sought to make the practices of the Midianites more comprehensible to his audience by substituting this designation for the older term strictly applicable to Gideon's period. But a confusion between Ishmaelites and Midianites occurs at an earlier moment in biblical narrative, when Joseph's brothers spot the caravan and hit on the idea of selling him into slavery. Without contradicting the conventional assignment of these two terms in Genesis to two different sources, E and J, I would like to propose an unconventional way of thinking about the use of the terms. Whatever the reasons for the working of both Ishmaelites and Midianites into the older story, I would suggest that the ancient audience was familiar with the conspicuous switch in designation in Genesis 37 and that a similar switch here, in conjunction with the peculiar prominence of the Midianite-Ishmaelite camels (it is a camel caravan in the Joseph story), may have been used as a marker of allusion. The recollection, however teasingly oblique, would set up a background of tension to the narrated events: a flickering memory of the moment of fraternal betrayal as the Israelites entreat Gideon to be their king. Joseph himself is a figure who climbs from slavery to royal status but is ultimately the king's high functionary and will found no dynasty.

If the connection with Joseph is a teasing possibility, the parallels to Moses and Aaron are emphatic. Gideon follows good theological doctrine in insisting that not he or his sons but the Lord alone should reign. His stance, though not his language, is reminiscent of Moses in the Wilderness tales, the Moses who eschews dynastic rule, who, like Samuel after him, vows that he has never expropriated a single donkey or otherwise exploited the people, as monarchs are wont to do (see, for example, Num. 38:15). Judges, however, is a constant chronicle of rapid decline, and that process can be seen here in the switch within the space of a verse from the model of Moses to that of Aaron at his weakest moment. In this regard, there is a silence at this point in our text that deserves commentary.

Let me propose a general formal principle of biblical narrative. In dialogue, in most instances in which a speaker com-

pletes a statement and then begins another statement with a
new "he said" (*wayomer*) formula of introduction, we are
invited to wonder why there is no intervening response from
the other party to the dialogue: has something inferable from
the narrative situation transpired in the silence between first
speech and second speech by the same character? What seems
to me likely in the exchange between Gideon and the men of
Israel is the silence of stubborn resistance. He makes the ring-
ing declaration that not he but the Lord will rule over them.
They look at him hard-eyed, unconvinced, and he realizes
that some other step is necessary. In the pattern of allusion,
what he does is to make the move from Moses to Aaron: the
request for golden earrings, precisely Aaron's request in the
episode of the Golden Calf (Exodus 32), is something concrete
and in a way reassuring that they can understand, as the
impatient Israelites in Exodus, perplexed by the imageless
God with whom Moses has tarried on the mountain, could
understand the graven image Aaron fashions out of their
gold. The people proclaim of the Golden Calf, "These are your
gods, O Israel, who brought you up from the land of Egypt."
This very phrase has been on Gideon's mind since the
encounter with the angel that initiates his vocation as judge:
"and where are his wonders of which our fathers told us, saying, 'Has not the Lord brought us up from Egypt?'" (Judg.
6:13).

The allusion to the Golden Calf provides a thematic link
between the political and the cultic questions at the end of the
Gideon story. From the gold earrings cast into the cloak (as
Aaron lamely told Moses, "I cast it into the fire and this calf
came out" [Exod. 32:24]), Gideon makes a cult object, an
ephod, which he sets up in his hometown, "and all Israel
whored after it there, and it was a snare for Gideon and his
household" (Judg. 8:27). In the writer's antimonarchic view,
the monarchy itself is a kind of idolatry. When Gideon sees

that the people are loath to do without it, he finds an equivalent that seems to him a lesser evil, a golden image, presumably to be used as an appurtenance of monotheistic cult, which will in its own way give the people a sense of security in its chronic historical anxiety, being a solid institution, as is monarchy, *kekhol hagoyim*, like those of all other nations. Just as the story of Gideon is about to round out to formulaic closure ("and the land was quiet forty years"), the "snare" of the cultic sin, against the background of the crisis of belief and leadership in the Golden Calf episode, introduces an ominous note that prepares us for the breakdown of order about to come. In the next story, Gideon's bastard son Abimelech will massacre his seventy half brothers, and in that tale of disaster we get a grim, monitory picture of the kind of gnarled, destructive person who would aspire to be king.

The examples we have considered do not, of course, exhaust the range of possibilities of allusive technique in biblical narrative, and they scarcely intimate the densely allusive character of biblical poetry, which often depends on a minute phrasal recall of earlier poems and narrative texts. But the three categories I have proposed—local allusion for the definition of theme, allusion dictated by actual continuity and narrative reenactment, allusion to models as part of an ideological argument—broadly mark the three most common occasions for allusion in biblical literature. In any case, the ubiquity of allusion in this body of texts tells us something important about the character of the literature cultivated in ancient Israel.

The diversity of biblical literature is one of its most remarkable features. Over the eight or more centuries during which it was created, as we turn from one genre to the next, one school to the next, and one era to the next, there are often startling changes not just in emphasis but in fundamental outlook, even vehement debate among writers. But for all this diversity, there is also a kind of elastic consensus that expresses itself in certain shared values and concepts, accompanied by a shared set of images, idioms, model figures, and exemplary stories. For all we know, there may have been a Hebrew literature that operated outside this consensus and that did not survive. Within the consensus, allusion was a natural means of reinforcing ideological continuity across schools and eras. It was a matter not, as some scholars have imagined, of mechanically reproducing literary material from the past but of elaborating, transforming, reversing, reinventing, or selectively remembering pieces of the past to fit into a new textual pattern.

This is what generally happens in the literary deployment of allusion, the difference being that certain notions of God, man, nature, and history that came to define national consciousness were locked into these habits of allusion. God's sovereign power seen as a transformation of primal chaos into order and the liberation from Egyptian bondage seen as the great sign of Israel's historical election were so central that writers of the most disparate aims and backgrounds repeatedly rang the changes on these ideas as they had been classically formulated in Genesis and Exodus, respectively. Allusion, then, becomes an index of the degree to which ancient Hebrew literature was on its way from corpus to canon, even if certain later institutional notions of canonization would have been alien to it. For the prominent play of allusion requires that the sundry texts be put together, taken together, seen, even in their sharp variety, as an overarching unity.

At the same time, allusion beautifully manifests what we have come to see increasingly in other formal aspects of literary technique in the Bible (such as repetition, ellipsis, dialogue, narrative point of view)—the imaginative subtlety, the extraordinary technical inventiveness, of the ancient Hebrew writers. It is, I think, a daring leap of imagination for a writer to put in the mouth of a man about to rape his sister the very words used in an earlier story by a man about to reveal himself to his brothers who have done him violence and presumed him dead. After that initial leap, it requires the most sophisticated awareness of the expressive possibilities of intertextual irony for the writer to develop as he does a fine network of links between the story he is telling and the tale once told of Joseph. These are, often quite spectacularly, narratives that deserve the most nicely attuned attention, not always in the same way but surely to the same degree as the modern classics of art fiction, from Flaubert to James and beyond. The delicate movement of allusion through the various biblical texts, sometimes perceptible in a single word, sometimes palpable in the large outlines of a story, abundantly demonstrates that for the Hebrew writers literary tradition was ultimately not the product of a pious compulsion, as scholarship has often pretended, but a resource to be drawn on again and again for the shifting expressive needs of a purposeful art.

CHAPTER 6

Literary Criticism
and the Problem of
Commentary

It is a revealing symptom of our cultural malaise that for two decades our academic institutions have been shaken by spasms of radical reevaluation of what we do with texts, ranging from uneasy self-doubt to incipient panic to the exhilaration of an intellectual witches' Sabbath. At this moment, even as the star of deconstruction begins to fade in the constellation of academic fashions, there is a lingering consensus that texts are highly unstable objects of knowledge, covertly asserting something other than what they seem to be saying, and that interpreters ineluctably betray texts by translating them, as they always must, into their own conceptual frameworks, epistemological assumptions, and implicit ideological aims. An instructive sign of the times was a major symposium on textual glosses held at the University of California Humanities Research Institute at Irvine in 1988. There was virtual agreement among participants—leading classicists, medievalists, and Renaissance scholars, with Jacques Derrida as de rigueur respondent—that no comment on a text is ever innocent, that every act of exegesis or even of ostensibly simple glossing is a means of intervening in the text, asserting power over it and over those who would use it.

Against this background, the publication of the first three volumes of an ambitious new commentary on the Pentateuch, sponsored by the Jewish Publication Society of America (JPS),[1] is a monument to the age of innocence of modern textual interpretation, which could be said to extend from the late eighteenth century until the mid-1960s. Innocence, however, does produce a kind of enabling procedural confidence in the act of explication, and all three commentaries actually demonstrate that some aspects of the text are susceptible to what we may still unblushingly call scientific investigation. At the same time, the commentaries raise a cluster of intriguing questions about what we can know about a text, especially an ancient text; about what it is useful to know, which may be quite another matter; and about the appropriate methods for undertaking the quest for knowledge.

Especially because I will later express some misgivings, let me say clearly at the outset that *The JPS Torah Commentary* is a scholarly achievement of a high order. It is probably the equal of the best volumes of the Anchor Bible that have appeared and exceeds that series in the balance of perspectives and the fullness of elucidation it provides. (Two of the contributors, it should be noted, Baruch A. Levine and Jacob Milgrom, have also been working on volumes that will appear in the Anchor series.) Altogether, *The JPS Torah Commentary* should long remain an invaluable tool for anyone seeking to come to grips with the Pentateuch in all its knotty philological and historical particularities.

This is neither a denominational commentary nor one especially suitable for synagogue use, in contrast to W. Gunther Plaut's admirable *The Torah: A Modern Commentary*, published a number of years ago by the Reform movement. It is a synthesis of the best of serious modern biblical scholarship, which has come more and more to transcend the theological or didactic assumptions of its denominational origins. The Jewish character of the JPS commentary is most visible in its abundant incorporation of insights from the Midrash and the medieval Hebrew exegetes (a topic to which we shall return), but pride of place is still accorded to the revelations of archaeology, comparative Semitic philology, ancient Near Eastern religions, and anthropology—all those trends in biblical research that I once designated as "excavative." In any case, the Jewish Publication Society clearly was impelled by a sense of forging a strong new link in the great chain of Jewish exegesis stretching back to late antiquity, as Nahum Sarna, general editor of the series, and Chaim Potok, its literary editor, stress in their manifesto.

In keeping with that perception of high purpose, the volumes have been sumptuously produced. The Hebrew text of the Leningrad Codex (the oldest dated manuscript of the entire Hebrew Bible), in handsome type, is printed in a parallel column alongside the text of the 1962 JPS translation of the Torah. The commentary, in smaller type below, stands in a ratio of roughly five or six to one to the Pentateuchal text. It includes not only glosses of terms and elucidations of difficulties but also observations on religious concepts, historical issues, compositional patterns, literary motifs, and much else. The biblical text is also broken down into small literary units, with prefatory remarks about each unit often running to several paragraphs. Each book of the Torah is presented with an introductory essay, and the body of the commentary is followed by a section called "Excursuses"—that is, extended notes, typically a page or two in length, on topics that could not be dealt with adequately within the confines of the commentary proper.

This entire format obviously has been carefully conceived, and I have only two quibbles. Because the volumes run from right to left, with the Hebrew text, the double columns of endnote references to the commentary are a little confusing to follow, and I often had to look at least twice before locating the right notes for the chapter. And though each contributor, as the editors inform us, was allowed the liberty of his own perspective, in Milgrom's use of excursuses the disproportion is bizarre—178 large, closely printed pages in comparison to 36 by Sarna and 40 by Levine. The result is that well over a third of Milgrom's volume is made up of what amounts to a small encyclopedia of biblical institutions and concepts. Much instructive matter is thereby conveyed, but one senses a palpable transgression of the strict purpose of commentary in the series as a whole.

It may be a coincidence that all three contributors have had an association with the Jewish Theological Seminary (JTS), the training institution of Conservative Judaism. Sarna taught there early in his career, and both Levine and Milgrom, though long based at universities, hold rabbinical degrees from JTS. (Sarna will also do Exodus for the series, while Deuteronomy has been assigned to Jeffrey Tigay of the University of Pennsylvania, a scholar with a background of expertise in ancient Near Eastern law and literature.) Levine and Milgrom both studied at JTS with H. L. Ginsberg, the great biblical philologist (as did Jeffrey Tigay), and the productive traces of his work can be detected in their commentaries.

Each of the commentators has his own forte, and each seems nicely matched with the text he expounds. Milgrom on Numbers exhibits a special mastery of cultic intricacies, though he also intelligently addresses a wide variety of other issues, and the reader will learn from his commentary all he is likely to want to know about how and why sacrificial blood is sprinkled on the altar, which orders of impurity are neutralized by which ritual gestures and substances, what numbers and kinds of animals are deemed appropriate for the sundry categories of offering. Levine on Leviticus is an accomplished Semitic philologist, and the discriminations he makes in the meanings of terms, their technical application, and the semantic fields from which they have been drawn, turn his commentary into a sustained lesson in the precise understanding of biblical Hebrew. All three commentators exhibit an impressive ability to bring together a broad range of learning pertinent to the Bible, but Sarna on Genesis is the aptest synthesizer among them, and that gift, happily brought to bear on the richest narrative material in the Torah, makes his volume the outstanding one of the three. Much of this understanding may not be new to scholarly eyes, but Sarna performs a valuable service to the nonspecialist in deftly bringing it all together. He offers a wealth of archaeological and comparative-historical information on the place-names, the genealogies, and the various indications of migration and conquest and cult location in Genesis, and at the same time he has a keen eye for the unifying compositional strategies, the recurring motifs, even some of the nuances of psychological motivation of the narratives. He also exhibits a good deal of exegetical tact, that fine sense of knowing when to be expansive and when to be terse, or not to comment at all. There are occasional exceptions, though: the genealogies in Genesis, which have exerted immeasurably greater fascination on historians than on ordinary readers, are accorded a good deal more space, with patient cross-referencing to cuneiform literature and archaeological digs, than the most humanly complex dramatic encounters in the Joseph story. The results of such inquiry are not illuminations but delectable curiosities, as when we are informed that the enigmatic Ashkenaz of Genesis 10:3, after which Central European Jewry took its name, is "doubtless identical with Ashkuzai or Ishkuza of Assyrian texts" and designates the same Indo-European people that the Greeks called the Scythians.

There is no unanimity among the three JPS commentators (any more than there was among the various medieval Hebrew exegetes). Sarna and Milgrom, following the precedent of E. A. Speiser a generation ago, are inclined to find evidence of the antiquity of the traditions embodied in their texts, while Levine stresses certain manifestly late accretions in Leviticus. Milgrom and Levine explicitly invoke the different strands or sources postulated by the Documentary Hypothesis, especially those sources designated P and D, while Sarna announces at the outset that "the Book of Genesis came down to us, not as a composite of disparate elements but as a unified document with a life, coherence, and integrity of its own." He then proceeds to write a commentary that makes an occasional discreet reference to an evident discontinuity in the text but prefers to invoke a unifying agency called "the Narrator," and—this surely constitutes a landmark in modern biblical scholarship—manages to dispense entirely with the source designations E, J, and P without seeming apologetic.

Other differences can be noted. For Milgrom the category of sacrifice known as *shelamim* is "a well-being offering," while Levine is confident in identifying it as a "gift of greeting," intended to be offered to the deity when the celebrant first enters the sanctuary. Sarna follows a modern scholarly consensus in interpreting *qedeshah* as a cult prostitute, whereas Milgrom is convinced that she provided cultic but not sexual services and that there was no cultic prostitution in the ancient Near East.

Finally, it should be noted that the commentators disagree

sometimes not only with each other but also, quite often, with the 1962 JPS translation that was conceived as the cornerstone of their joint enterprise. With a heavy heart, I am compelled to say after reading them that it will soon be time for a completely new translation. Few readers have been tempted to defend the JPS version on grounds of stylistic felicity, and I can attest that it repeatedly obscures or distorts features of the literary art of the original. Its great claims to authority were clarity and painstaking philological precision, but in the light of *The JPS Torah Commentary*, even that begins to look shaky. Sarna occasionally rejects a decision of the translation; Milgrom and, even more, Levine differ with the JPS translators repeatedly, sometimes quite emphatically.

At certain points, the divergences are grotesque. Thus, the JPS translation renders the mysterious term *'orot teḥashim*, a material used as an outer covering of the wilderness tabernacle, as "dolphin skins"—where would they have gotten hold of those in the Sinai?—while Milgrom, citing proposed cognates in Sumerian and Hurrian, reads it as "orange-yellow skins." The JPS translates Leviticus 10:2 as follows: "And fire came forth from the LORD and consumed them; thus they died at the instance of the LORD." The last phrase purports to represent the Hebrew *lifney YHWH* and reflects the JPS mania for translating literal utterances as special idioms or abstractions. Levine justly notes that the phrase means here what it generally means elsewhere, "before the Lord": especially since the subsequent verses are concerned with the removal of the bodies from the sanctuary, what we have is a simple indication of place, not some fancy-footwork reference to agency.

Against the challenge of "the hermeneutics of suspicion" (Paul Ricoeur's phrase) prevalent in the humanities today, is it conceivable that a commentary can ever enlarge our understanding of a text, as opposed simply to providing another understanding? Texts, to begin with, are made up of words, and any attempt to come to grips with the range of possible meanings of the text must begin by registering the precise nuances of the words used. Recovering lexical nuances becomes a task for any text written more than a generation ago, and it obviously has special urgency for an ancient text.

In the field of biblical research, where since the nineteenth century such a wealth of inscriptions, continuous texts, and precious fragments in previously unknown languages has been uncovered, the semantic insights of comparative philology have been particularly valuable, as *The JPS Torah Commentary* repeatedly demonstrates. There are always many feasible readings for any text, and the biblical text itself often makes dizzying use of the ambiguities of certain terms, but we can carry out our many readings more responsibly now because we understand much more clearly the meanings of the Hebrew words.

In many instances, it turns out that seemingly general terms refer precisely to specific ancient Near Eastern institutions or legal practices. Thus, the "liberty" proclaimed to all the inhabitants of the land in the jubilee year (Lev. 25:10), and duly inscribed in that embracing sense on the Liberty Bell, is rendered "release" in the 1962 JPS translation, with good reason, as Baruch Levine explains: "Hebrew *deror* is cognate with Akkadian *andarūu*, which designates an edict of release issued by the Old Babylonian kings and some of their successors." This edict was part of a general "moratorium declared on debts and indenture." In Genesis 21, when Abimelech resolves a dispute over wells by making Abraham swear that the Hebrew pastoralist will not "deal falsely" (*tishqor*) with him, he is doing more than making a plea for honest treatment. As Sarna observes, this verb, which appears biblically only here in this particular conjugation, "occurs repeatedly in the 8th-century B.C.E. Sfire treaty with the specific technical sense of being guilty of a breach of contractual obligation."

The term, then, is not merely an exhortation but what linguists call a performative utterance, ratifying through the act of enunciation, as Sarna concludes, "a pact of mutual nonaggression."

At times, comparative philology provides an almost microscopic clarity of definition for hitherto poorly understood terms, as when Levine instructs us that the rare Hebrew noun *peder,* "suet," which occurs only twice in the Bible, both times in Leviticus, "is cognate with the Akkadian *pitru,* a term used in cuneiform texts, where it refers to the loose covering of fat over the liver." Elsewhere, linguistic comparison yields a nuance of implication for a familiar word. *Ne`arim,* which generally means "lads" or "servants," also has a military sense, as is clear in its usage in the battle scenes in 1 and 2 Samuel. Sarna proposes that in its occurrence in Genesis 14, at the end of Abram's campaign against the alliance of four kings, the meaning is "warriors," noting that "the word is found in Egyptian as *ne`arin,* a borrowing from the Canaanite in the specialized sense of 'elite corps.'" Or again, *mela'khah,* one of several biblical terms for "work," is shown by Levine to have the nuance of "assigned tasks, what one is sent to do," because it can be linked with the verbal root *l-'-k,* "to send, dispatch, assign," not found in the Bible but occurring in Ugaritic texts. This throws into sharper focus the cognate noun *mal'akh,* "messenger" or "angel"—as, for example, the *mal'akhim,* surely no angels, whom Saul dispatches as hit men to murder David in 1 Samuel 18.

Beyond such purely lexical considerations, the abundant recourse of the commentaries to excavative scholarship often helps us recover a sense of the concrete historical contexts in which these stories were enacted and these laws pronounced. Thus, in connection with the episode of the copper serpent in Numbers 21, Milgrom notes that a five-inch-long copper serpent has actually been found at Timna, the copper mine near

the Gulf of Aqaba and apparently the region in which the biblical tale is set, dating from about the same period. The indications are that such serpents were used as cult objects by
nomadic tribes in this area. Sarna elucidates the mysterious
hacking in two of animals in the covenant between God and
Abram in Genesis 15 by again citing the Sfire treaty, in which
the cutting up of animals is explicitly named as "a form of self-
imprecation"—what will be the fate of the signatories if they
betray the terms of the treaty. In other instances, the invocation
of ancient Near Eastern backgrounds involves more of a leap
of inference, but even then it has the effect of opening up possibilities for interpretive consideration, as when Sarna proposes that the shame over nakedness in Genesis 3 obliquely
reflects a protest "against pagan fertility cults and a reaction
against a Near Eastern practice of priests, as in Sumer, where
the cultic ritual was performed in the nude."

In all these respects, the JPS commentary reads like any
other scholarly exegesis of the Bible, though a case could be
made that it is an unusual synthesis of such scholarship. Its
one distinguishing trait is the frequent use of traditional
Jewish commentaries, from the Midrashim of late antiquity
through the great medieval exegetes, beginning with Saadia
in the tenth century, down to Samuel David Luzzato in nineteenth-century Italy. (Most biblical scholars would not have
access to the majority of these commentaries, because they
would have great difficulty reading postbiblical Hebrew.)
The invocation of these sundry sources is more than a gesture
of Jewish patriotism, though it also makes an implicit ideological affirmation: the Jews have been one continuous people,
from biblical origins to modernity, cherishing a special relation to these great texts of their origins. It is noteworthy in
this regard that Levine appends to his commentary a twenty-
one-page essay entitled "Leviticus in the Ongoing Jewish
Tradition."

Beyond such linking of the Torah to the subsequent historical experience of the Jewish people, one of the contributors, Jacob Milgrom, after affirming his intention to be "critical, unapologetic, and objective," makes the astonishing theological claim that his commentary "offers reliable support to those who believe that this book and the Torah at large were divinely revealed." It is hard to imagine what in his commentary, including the citation of Jewish sources, he thinks might confirm this claim. In fact, his painstaking accounts of trial by ordeal, ritual contamination by corpses and menstruants, hovering miasmas of impurity, the rite of the scapegoat, and much else bring us almost uncomfortably close to a thoroughly alien world in which pagan and magical notions have undergone no more than a first phase of monotheistic transformation. But quite apart from such odd gestures to the faithful, the central Jewish feature of the JPS commentary— referring to the traditional exegetes—has an intrinsic justification in the enterprise of understanding the text. Indeed, it raises the question of whether there is such a thing as cumulative knowledge in the study of texts, and the JPS commentary offers a good deal of support for an affirmative answer.

The Bible—and the Pentateuch in particular—as the text of our culture most intimately associated with moral, theological, and even historical authority, has through the centuries been our most heavily studied book, by Jews and Christians alike. I would contend, however, that until modern times Jews and Christians scrutinized the Hebrew Bible with different orders of attention. The reasons for the difference were both theological and linguistic. Jews always conceived this corpus as a textual object complete in itself, addressing the life of a people in real historical time, and not as a typological forerunner to another group of books composed in a different language, pointing through figures and parables to a posthistorical end time. (Rabbinic literature, to be sure, had its own typological reading of the Bible, but it never claimed for itself the status of canonical completion or supersession of the Hebrew Bible, as did the New Testament.) Jews also always investigated the Bible in its original language, and in sharp contrast to the occasional manifestations of Christian Hebraism, they preserved Hebrew as a living language of study and inner experience even when it was no longer a vernacular.[2]

Thus, the sundry Midrashim composed between the fourth and the ninth centuries C.E., though they often propose readings that may seem fanciful to the modern eye, exhibit the most remarkable acuteness in identifying connotations and nuances of difference in Hebrew terms. I would suggest that this repeated demonstration of insight into the language is a consequence not of happy intuition but of active participation in a continuous tradition that carried over a finely shaded knowledge of biblical Hebrew into the era of changed rabbinic usage. That tradition, variously refracted but also reinvigorated by the invention of philology and the poetic revival begun in medieval Andalusia, is still palpable in the fine linguistic discriminations of Abraham Ibn Ezra (twelfth-century Spain, Italy, and France), David Kimhi (twelfth-and thirteenth-century France), and Rashi (eleventh-century France). These were all brilliant readers, but also readers with a deep and ramified rootage in a historically continuous Hebrew culture.

All three of the JPS commentaries provide abundant instances in which the traditional exegetes anticipated specific conclusions of modern scholarship. At least in the effort to understand the plain meaning of the words of the text, they did not belong to a remote, benighted world of naïve believers but were joined in the same enterprise, without benefit of Akkadian and Ugaritic, as the latter-day sages of Göttingen and Harvard and Johns Hopkins. Thus, Milgrom comments on a difficult term, *dalyav*, in an enigmatic image that appears in Balaam's oracular poem (Num. 24:7). Both Ibn Ezra and Luzzato construe it as a variant form of *daliyotav*, "its boughs," whereas "Rashi says that the form of the word is dual and can mean 'buckets' [that is, deriving the term from *deli*, "bucket"]." He goes on to quote Rashi's elucidation of the image in the poem: a man with two full buckets, the water splashing over the rims as he walks back from the well. To which Milgrom adds, making medieval exegete and modern Semiticist join hands, "In support, Akkadian *dalû* means 'irrigate with water drawn from a well.'"

The JPS Torah Commentary, then, offers a wealth of resources to the serious student of the Bible, but at least intermittently, it suffers from an inclination to perpetuate the legacy of positivism of modern biblical scholarship going back to nineteenth-century Germany (one might recall here Milgrom's confidence in the possibility of an "objective" commentary). The cognitive model for this whole modern enterprise of commentary is, I think, the textual crux. One encounters a difficult place in the text, something that does not make sense. With great patience and a little luck—perhaps something unearthed by the archaeologist's spade or a suddenly grasped phonetic connection between an obscure biblical word and a term in a Sumerian text—the crux may be solved. Characteristically, all three commentators often invoke the formula that, in the present state of knowledge, the text in question cannot yet be understood. The Bible as a whole is conceived as an intricate edifice of *puzzlements*—philological, compositional, historical—that one by one require solutions and with a combination of ingenuity and serendipity will get them. What these commentators and their many modern forerunners do not readily imagine is that much biblical writing—I am, of course, not speaking of what scribes may have inadvertently interposed—might have been devised precisely not to yield a solution, or to yield multiple and contradictory solutions, and that this might be the very hallmark of its greatness. Let me cite an example from Sarna, because in most respects he is the most subtle and the most resourceful of the three commentators.

In a 1,300-word excursus on the topic "Jacob's Struggle with the Angel," Sarna first usefully associates the story with the widespread folktale of the inimical river spirit who opposes a traveler seeking to cross over into his territory, duly noting how the biblical writer has transformed this common material for his own, monotheistic purposes. He then cites the venerable Midrash that sees the nameless adversary as "the celestial patron of Esau" (*saro shel Esav*) and argues for the plausibility of that identification. "In summation, the mysterious creature who assails Jacob as he is about to cross the future border of Israel is none other than the celestial patron of Esau-Edom, who is the inveterate enemy of Israel." This conclusion is not so much wrong as wrongly put. The story of Jacob's wrestling with the angel, one of the most haunting in all of ancient literature, is conceived as a puzzle awaiting a solution, like some poorly understood Hebrew term, *peder* or *deror*.

Most readers will share the sense that Jacob's grappling in the night with a mysterious "man" by the ford of the Jabbok, before the morning when he will see his estranged brother after a twenty-year separation, is an adumbration of the imminent encounter between the twins. But is that adumbration a political allegory, as the Midrash has it, or a night-world expression of Jacob's psychology, or an experience of the dangerous, inscrutable ambiguity of the divine that touches on yet also transcends the story of fraternal conflict? Can we be entirely sure, despite the twin traditions of exegesis and iconography, that the nameless adversary is actually an angel and not God himself? By proclaiming that the angel is "none other than" Esau's celestial patron, the commentary reduces the biblical tale to a simple linearity that impoverishes it.

In *The Genesis of Secrecy*, the literary critic Frank Kermode suggestively juxtaposes the enigmatic young man in the white shirt in the Gospel according to Mark with the elusive man in the brown mackintosh in Joyce's *Ulysses* in order to argue that a certain kind of narrative works its art by withholding some of its own key meanings. Historical exegesis of the Bible tends to presuppose "solutions," but literary exegesis, which Sarna himself also practices, and at times quite ably, must be able to respect the secrecy of the Bible—not by enjoining silence but by articulating an order of commentary that will help readers tune in to the multiple reverberations of the secrets.

Both Sarna and Milgrom devote considerable attention, often literary in character, to the microscopic level of word choices and isolable motifs and to the macroscopic level of compositional patterns through which smaller narrative segments are woven together. (I leave Levine out of this consideration because there is such limited narrative material in Leviticus.) What is neglected is the crucial middle ground in which literary analysis might consider the stylistic realization and the technical narrative options employed, as motifs are fleshed out and patterns translated into particular acts and speeches and gestures. What happens on this middle ground makes all the difference in the kinds of meanings suggested by the text.

Thus, on the first of the three occasions when the story of the sister bride is told in Genesis (Chapter 12), Sarna comments, "According to the literary concepts and norms of the ancient world, reiteration is a desirable and characteristic feature of the epic tradition. To the biblical Narrator, repetition of the experience serves to emphasize and reinforce his didactic purposes." This is not altogether wrong, but it is too general and a little fuzzy, especially in the vague invocation of "the epic tradition" in relation to Genesis, and in its assumption that these stories are didactic. (Meir Sternberg, one of several recent literary critics of the Bible whom Sarna repeatedly cites in his notes, has made the persuasive distinction that biblical narrative has ideological aims but is never merely didactic.)[3] If one looks carefully at the narrative articulation of the three sister-bride stories, it becomes clear that instead of simple repetition for emphasis, each version is worked out in consonance with its own context to achieve different thematic ends. This procedure of significant variation in seeming repetition is itself one of the distinctive features of the Bible's narrative art.

The first version, set at the very beginning of the sequence of Patriarchal tales, is the most succinct of the three and does everything possible to maximize the force of the story as a foreshadowing of the sojourn in Egypt that will be the fate of Abraham's progeny (an idea already noted in the Midrash). Abram and Sarai go down to Egypt because there is a "heavy famine" in the land. Abram is afraid that the Egyptians will kill him while her "they will let live," just as Pharaoh in Exodus decrees that all the males born will be thrown into the Nile while all the female babies "you will let live." When Pharaoh in Genesis 12 takes Sarai into his harem, God intervenes by afflicting him with plagues, and Pharaoh then peremptorily "sends away" Abram and Sarai, the same verb of dismissal or release repeatedly used in the Exodus narrative.

The second version of the sister-bride story in Genesis 20 takes place not in Egypt but in Gerar, in the northwestern Negev, and it is in no way aligned with the sojourn in Egypt. This time there is no mention of a famine. Abimelech is most unpharaonic in appearing as a man of conscience, more sinned against than sinning, whose castigation of Abraham for deceiving him about Sarah's identity momentarily puts the patriarch at a loss for words (see the significant silence between verses 9 and 10). He is vouchsafed a night-vision colloquy with God, and the odd phrase he uses in challenging God, "Will you also slay a righteous people?" pointedly makes a link between this story and the immediately preceding one, the destruction of Sodom. In this version, Abraham imagines Gerar is another Sodom—a place where if two strangers appear (in this instance, one male and one female) at least one of them is likely to be subject to sexual assault and the other to murder. In the event, he is quite wrong about the moral character of Gerar, and one of the purposes of this episode seems to be a desire to unsettle any simple Hebrew/Gentile polarity. Finally, the remission of the plague of sterility—rereading, we realize it is probably a plague of impotence, hinted at in God's words to Abimelech, "Therefore I did not let you touch her"—about which we learn only at the very end of the story, connects the whole episode both with the concern about procreation that dominates Chapter 18 and the second half of Chapter 19 and with Sarah's long-deferred conception, which is announced in the next verse (the beginning of Chapter 21).

The third version of the story, in Genesis 26, involving Isaac and Rebekah, is sandwiched between Esau's selling of the birthright to Jacob and Jacob's theft of the paternal blessing. It is not surprising that much of the articulation of the sister-bride tale here is attuned to the themes of inheritance and blessing. Although famine is again the motive for migration, the place of refuge is Gerar, not Egypt, and it is stressed that the area is part of the promised land of inheritance. Only here is a reiteration of the covenantal promise of blessing and great progeny inserted in the story (verses 3–5), and here the patriarch with his wife is not sent out or driven away but, on the contrary, proceeds to plant crops and tend flocks in territory contiguous with or overlapping the kingdom of Gerar.

In this version, Abimelech learns of the matriarch's status as wife not through divine intervention in plague or night vision but by peering out the window and seeing Isaac "fondling" Rebekah—*metsaḥeq*, the word motif that has been following Isaac, Yitsḥaq, from before his conception. This matriarch is never actually taken into the harem, but is only in danger of being appropriated by the king—perhaps a reflection of Rebekah's powerful and active character in contradistinction to that of the more passive Sarah. Here the wealth that accrues to the patriarch is not a gift from the king—as in the Exodus story, when the fleeing Hebrews "despoil" the Egyptians—but the result of his activity as agriculturalist and pastoralist, an anticipation of the precise terms of the blessing that Isaac will confer on Jacob and that Jacob will realize later in his dealings with Laban. Finally, despite Sarna's claim that the story "temporarily diverts attention from the ongoing rivalry between Jacob and Esau," this version, in contrast to the two earlier ones, actually concludes with an episode that ties in firmly with the overarching theme of fraternal strife and the struggle for the inheritance: the shepherds of Abimelech quarrel with Isaac's shepherds over wells; and Abimelech is impelled to tell Isaac that he must move off, "for you have become far too big for us," just as the reconciled Jacob and Esau later will separate because the great camp of Jacob's family and possessions requires its own space.

The lack of adequate attention to this middle ground of the literary articulation of the narratives is sometimes detrimentally combined by the modern exegetes with a positivist faith in the invocation of a legal, social, or cultic institution as in itself sufficient reason for a proposed reading. It is, of course, essential to understand what are the ancient institutions that play various roles in the narratives, and in this regard the JPS commentators give readers much useful guidance, but it is quite another thing to assume that recognition of the institution provides an automatic key to the meaning of the story. Let me illustrate this pitfall with a final example, which, as it happens, takes us beyond the frame of the Pentateuch.

Milgrom, at the end of an excursus explaining the ritual conditions of *ḥerem*, the biblical ban of general destruction, cites the story of the conflict between Samuel and Saul in 1 Samuel 15 over the ban Samuel had enjoined against the Amalekites. Milgrom contends that in fact Saul, after defeating the Amalekites, was punctiliously observing the conditions of the *ḥerem*, bringing back only unblemished animals eligible for sacrifice and in all likelihood intending to slaughter the Amalekite king Agag "before the Lord" as Samuel proceeded to do at the end of the story. According to Milgrom, the fact that Saul is said to lose his kingship without further appeal because of his behavior here must be attributed to the *Tendenz* of the "Davidide (that is, anti-Saulide) author."

Such pseudo-historical, quasi-scientific labeling has been a bane of biblical scholarship for over a century. Is there any plausible evidence that there was ever such an animal as a "Davidide author"? It has been comforting to biblical scholars to hypothesize the existence of ideologically definite, politically demarcated "schools" of writers, and it takes no more than the smallest hint of a political viewpoint to justify such conjectural constructs. The biblical art of characterization makes these ideological attributions highly dubious. Throughout 1 and 2 Samuel the attitudes toward David are so complex, and David himself is represented as such a multifaceted, calculating, devious, and at times morally dubious figure, though also on occasion an appealing one, that any hypothesis of "Davidide" authorship looks questionable in the extreme.

But what about the nicely discriminated narrative data, the revelatory movement of dialogue, in the story itself as it is

worked out in 1 Samuel 15? The rounds of query and
response between prophet and king, as Meir Sternberg has
demonstrated in *The Poetics of Biblical Narrative*, show a Saul
painfully floundering, at first greeting Samuel with a bald-
faced lie, then progressively qualifying his statements as
Samuel verbally corners him, and finally confessing his transgression, begging Samuel at least to help him save face before
his assembled troops.[4] This is hardly the performance of a
man confident that he has scrupulously observed the institutional requirements of the ban.

Saul's self-incrimination can be illustrated with one small
strategic point not touched on by Sternberg. When Saul tri-
umphs over the Amalekites, the narrator reports his actions in
the following words: "And Saul and the people [or, troops]
spared Agag and the best of the flock and the cattle and the
second born and the lambs and all that was good, and they
did not want to put them to the ban." A nicety of biblical
grammar here should be noted. The verb *spared* is in the singular in the Hebrew, despite the plural subject, in conformity
with a general biblical usage that allows a singular verb when
one of the elements of a compound subject is considered the
primary actor, the others somehow subsidiary. (This point of
grammar was already observed by the medieval Hebrew
commentators.) The grammar thus informs us that it is Saul
who did the sparing, with the people merely following his
lead. When, however, Saul responds to Samuel's demand
that he explain the bleating of sheep and the braying of oxen
behind him, these are the words he uses: "From the
Amalekites they brought them, for the people spared the best
of the flock and the cattle in order to sacrifice to the Lord your
God, and the rest we put to the ban."

The little dance from third-person plural to third-person
singular to first-person plural is the desperate movement of a

guilty liar stumbling over his own feet. First, it is an impersonal "they" who are responsible for bringing the sheep and oxen from the Amalekites. Then, it is the people who "spared" the flocks: the singular verb used before by the narrator is now in perfect accord with its collective subject, but Saul's report entirely suppresses the narrator's firm indication that the king, not the people, was the primary instigator of the sparing. Finally, it is only when Saul speaks of putting the other, more meager animals to the ban that he switches to "we." The narrator's account had said nothing of setting aside the choice animals for the express purpose of sacrifice. At the very least, we are entitled to question the honesty of this purportedly pious motive now introduced by Saul. It is noteworthy that he speaks uneasily of sacrifice "to the Lord *your* God," not quite the tone that would be taken by a man sure he has been performing his solemn obligations before his own God and the God of his people.

Let me hasten to add that this cunning choreography of language in the passage does not provide a "solution" to the episode, as the legal stipulations of the institution of *ḥerem* are purported to do. Milgrom feels free to speak of "Saul's true intention," but a scrutiny of the literary articulation of the story leads us instead to the perception of a complex of plausible motives, not to a bedrock of truth, which in fact the story is devised to avoid. Saul himself, like most of the major biblical characters, remains elusive, a politically and psychologically persuasive conjunction of suggestive contradictions: inept, foolishly impulsive, self-doubting, pathetically unfit for kingship, and also a heroic and poignant figure, equally victimized by Samuel and by circumstances, sustained by a kind of lumbering integrity even as he entangles himself in a net of falsehood and self-destructive acts. The greatness of the story resides in this rich tension of internal opposition in the characterization, and the last thing a commentary should do is to dissolve the tension by invoking the simplifying hypothesis of an "anti-Saulide author."

In all this, I do not mean to suggest that the historical-philological and the literary approaches to the Bible are mutually contradictory undertakings. On the contrary, the exacting deployment of broad learning in the JPS commentaries demonstrates how much literary students of the Bible can refine their own analysis by attending to what the cumulative enterprise of scholarship has discovered about the meanings of biblical words, the nature of biblical institutions, the intricate tapestry of ancient historical contexts, and the possibilities of sedimentation and sutures in the texts. Many of the historical scholars, for their part, still need to understand better that a literary text—even an ancient and canonical one—is more than the broken pieces of a potsherd in an archaeological find to be fitted together like a jigsaw puzzle. At least to the extent that the redacted text forms a coherent continuity, and it usually does in the Bible, it is artfully contrived, as are literary texts from other times and places, to open up a dense swarm of variously compelling possibilities, leading us to ponder the imponderables of individual character, human nature, historical causation, revelation, election, and man's encounters with the divine. If all literary texts are open-ended, the Bible, certainly in its narrative aspect, is willfully, provocatively open-ended: that, indeed, is why there is always room for more commentary.

CHAPTER 7

The Quest for
the Author

One of the difficulties we as modern readers have assimilating the Bible to our habitual notions of literary expression is the stubborn resistance it offers to our readerly or critical need for an informing authorial presence with which we can contend. The tradition of Western literature is to a large extent framed by the conspicuous personalities of its major authors and their acts of self-assertion. The great emblem of this framing is Dante, who places himself in the foreground of his magisterial work and chooses his Latin epic forerunner Virgil as his guide within the narrative. Milton, in turn, will align himself with both Virgil and Dante (as well as with Tasso and others), and, still later, Joyce will explicitly define his own enterprise against the background of this whole sequence of epic poets, going back beyond Virgil to Homer. If the tradition that has formed our ideas of literature highlights in this way the persona or even the personality of the author, what are we to do with a set of ancient narratives that aspire to speak out of the void in an authoritative voice that masks any authorial presence? Perhaps prudence might prompt us to be content with the artifice and let alone the inaccessible artificer, but to a few contemporary critics excavative scholarship of the Bible seems to offer a tool for uncovering the lost author. The most spectacular recent effort of this sort has been undertaken by Harold Bloom, a critic long devoted to scrutinizing the forceful assertion of personality in literary expression.

Bloom has provoked, as he clearly intended, a storm of excitement, consternation, and ire by proposing that the so-called J writer, usually thought to be responsible for the earliest strand of the Pentateuch, was a woman. The project of *The Book of J*,[1] a work done in collaboration with the poet David Rosenberg, who has provided the translations of the biblical texts, bears a curious relation to that of Samuel Butler's quirky book published in 1897, *The Authoress of the Odyssey*. Bloom makes no mention of Butler, but there is some kinship between the lines of argumentation of the two books. Bloom, however, is after bigger game than the mere discovery of the gender of a revered ancient writer masked in anonymity.

There is no reason to be startled at the possibility that J was a woman, a possibility also put forth—tentatively and cautiously—by Richard Elliott Friedman in *Who Wrote the Bible?*[2] One might suppose that such an idea would be inspired by contemporary feminism, though Bloom actually positions himself as virtually an adversary of that movement, at least in its academic variant. As he spins out the hypothesis with his characteristic verve, wit, and flair for the unexpected, the hypothesis at moments becomes a beguiling one. We know very little about the education given the two sexes in ancient Israel, but both archaeological evidence and certain indications in the biblical texts themselves suggest that literacy was quite widespread, and there are certainly no grounds for excluding altogether the idea that one or more of the biblical authors may have been female. What Samuel Butler roundly declared of the *Odyssey* is equally apt for the writings designated by scholarship as J: "It may be urged that it is extremely improbable that any woman in any age should write such a masterpiece as the Odyssey. But so it also is that any man should do so." Thus, I do not think the claim that J was a woman is susceptible of refutation—a statement that can be made, incidentally, of many a latter-day theory about the Bible. However, what motivates Bloom to make the claim and what evidence he offers to support it (two rather different considerations) are questions worth pursuing.

But before confronting these compelling issues of how we are to conceive of authorship in the Bible, I am obliged to raise the painful question of the relation of *The Book of J* to the Hebrew text of the Bible. Bloom has made a catastrophic decision in tying his project to the translation of David Rosenberg. (The book as a whole comprises about 110 pages in large type of the Rosenberg translation and double that number of closely printed pages devoted to Bloom's introductions and commentaries.) There is abundant evidence that when Bloom talks about J he is actually referring to Rosenberg's English version of J, and the distance between the two is very considerable.

The first, and lesser, problem is an aesthetic one. J—who as Richard Friedman properly notes, is not really distinguishable from the Pentateuchal source E stylistically—writes wonderfully compact, beautifully cadenced Hebrew, using a supple, predominantly paratactic syntax and adhering, it is safe to assume, with nice precision to the idiomatic norms of the ancient language. Rosenberg's English is often syntactically choppy and elliptic and rhythmically bumpy, making abundant use of dashes, sometimes sounding like a weak imitation of Leopold Bloom's telegraphic style in *Ulysses*, and shuttling between past and present tenses in inscrutable ways for which the Hebrew offers scant justification. As for idiomatic usage, here are a few characteristic instances of Rosenberg's ear for English: Genesis 18:11, "Sarah no longer had her woman's flow" (literally, "the way of women") is conveyed as "The periods of women ceased to exist." The oracle about Jacob and Esau, "the elder will serve the younger," is represented as "youth grows senior over age." The biblical idiom of polite deference or subservience, "if I have found favor in your eyes," is rendered as "if your heart be warmed," which not only fails as English usage but also introduces an element of emotionality quite alien to the Hebrew expression of ancient politesse in a hierarchical social order.

More gravely, Rosenberg repeatedly misconstrues biblical terms or attaches arbitrary meanings to them. The "taskmasters" of the Exodus story incongruously turn into "policemen" in his version—the meaning the word has been assigned in modern Hebrew. The "city square" (*reḥov*) in which the angels visiting Sodom offer to spend the night is converted into a "broad road," something for which, given the ground plan of Canaanite cities, there could be no conceivable place in a built-up town. Without any philological warrant, the Hebrew for "evil," *ra`ah*, is repeatedly rendered as "contempt," a choice that Bloom somehow fancies as a great discovery of Rosenberg's, pointing to J's artistic aims. The Hebrew *tsedeq*, "justice," "righteousness," and, in some poetic texts, "victory," is unaccountably translated as "tolerance." And the list could go on and on of instances in which Rosenberg's English equivalents of the Hebrew are freewheeling inventions or downright misprisions.

His truly lethal tactic as translator, however, and the one on which Bloom builds most, is his decision to make his version a loose—poetic?—variation on the original or an interpretive paraphrase of it. J (like E) is one of the most chastely concise, brilliantly understated writers in the whole Western tradition. He, or she, steadily resists the emotive term, the explicit judgment, the self-explication, the effusive lyric gesture. Alas, these are all traits that Rosenberg promiscuously embraces. In his version, Cain is not "a wanderer and a fugitive in the earth" but "homeless as the blowing wind"—another phrase Bloom cites with relish as though it were in the Hebrew, as though J might really have some stylistic affinity with Bob Dylan. God in Genesis 12 does not just "afflict Pharaoh with great afflictions" but does it "as if with lightning." The maiden Rebekah, "very fair in appearance," is turned into a heroine of romance fiction when she is represented as "lovely as an apparition, as fresh." The burning bush is not simply "this great sight" but "this luminous thing." The enemies of the Lord in the incantation for the transportation of the ark in Numbers do not merely "scatter" but "disappear like stars." Thus, the spareness in the use of metaphor that is a hallmark of J's genius is sunk in a poetaster's fondness for metaphorical clichés.

It is baffling that a man of Harold Bloom's intelligence should be guilty of so extreme a lapse in taste, even without the ability to judge the philological issues, as to endorse this translation. What is disturbing is that his construction of J is far too often based on things in Rosenberg undreamt of in J's philosophy. Let me cite an extended example, one that Bloom himself remarks on in detail at the end of his introduction. He quotes in their entirety four English versions of the Tower of Babel story—Tyndale, the King James Version, E. A. Speiser's 1964 translation, and Rosenberg's—in order to demonstrate Rosenberg's superiority in conveying the subtle literary art of J. Here is the Rosenberg version:

Now listen: all the earth uses one tongue, one and the same words. Watch: they journey from the east, arrive at a valley in the land of Sumer, settle there.

"We can bring ourselves together," they said, "like stone on stone, use brick for stone: bake it until hard." For mortar they heated bitumen.

"If we bring ourselves together," they said, "we can build a city and tower; its top touching the sky—to arrive at fame. Without a name we're unbound, scattered over the face of the earth."

Yahweh came down to watch the city and the tower the sons of man were bound to build. "They are one people with the same tongue," said Yahweh. "They conceive this between them, and it leads up until no boundary exists to what they will touch. Between us, let's descend, baffle their tongue until each is scatter-brain to his friend."

From there Yahweh scattered them over the whole face of the earth; the city there came unbound.

That is why they named the place Bavel; their tongues were baffled there by Yahweh. Scattered by Yahweh, from there, they arrived at the ends of the earth.

Aesthetic considerations aside, this is less an English version of the original than a prefabricated interpretation masquerading as a translation. The bringing ourselves together, with the stones and bricks as a simile for the act of unification, is nowhere to be seen in the Hebrew, and no Hebrew stones clutter this Mesopotamian plain. Bloom speaks of the "dramatic irony" in J's use of the phrase "between us," though that phrase does not exist in the Hebrew text, which has only a first-person plural, "let us go down." Most grievously, Bloom waxes enthusiastic over "Rosenberg's care in repeating the subtle J's play upon 'bound,' 'boundary,' 'unbound.'" The fact of the matter is that there is not a *single word* in the nine verses of the Hebrew original that suggests either "bound" or "boundary." Although most of the biblical writers were indeed virtuosos in wordplay, as recent literary analysis has repeatedly shown, the only wordplay here that has a basis in J is "baffle"/"Bavel" (the rather feeble "scatterbrain"/"scatter" is still another interpolation of Rosenberg's). The translator, in other words, has decided that the theme of the story is the violation of boundaries, and through his own, heavyhanded puns he has "thematized" this perception in the text—the very last thing that would be done by so magisterially laconic a writer as J.

Such comments as these by Bloom on Rosenberg lead me to the reluctant conclusion that Bloom could not possibly be reading the Bible in the original. He does appear to have enough Hebrew to consult lexicons, not always with great profit, and at one point he provides a translation of his own, which I assume he must have done by looking at existing English versions with some inspection of the Hebrew. But since he does repeatedly refer to Hebrew terms, I am compelled to say that his allusions to Hebrew often betray an ignorance of the language—something that sets his project off from that of Samuel Butler, whose classical Greek was evidently quite sound.

J is several times called by Bloom a *gevurah* in Rehoboam's royal court, a term he thinks has the meaning "grand lady." But *gevirah* is the word for "grand lady," whereas *gevurah* can only be an abstract noun, meaning "power" or "bravery." The effect is like that of having a French writer tell us that Sir Philip Sidney was a "mastery," or *grand seigneur*, at the court of Elizabeth. Bloom follows Rosenberg in imagining that *nefesh"*—life force," "vital spirit," "essential self," and occasionally "gullet"—can also mean "flesh," something that would make gibberish of the declaration in Deuteronomy that "the blood is the *nefesh."* He is similarly led astray by his translator in claiming that the root *'rr,* a clear Hebrew term for "curse" and repeatedly used as a flat antithesis to "bless," really means "to bind" (apparently a confusion with the root *'sr).* He informs us that in the phrase "like smoke from the kiln" after the incineration of Sodom, "we are intended to remember the fiery kiln of the covenant vision" in Genesis 15, though in fact entirely unrelated Hebrew terms are used in the two texts. Above all, he repeatedly insists on the aptness of phrases that incorporate Rosenberg's adjectival and adverbial ornamentation, and on wordplay that is all Rosenberg's— conservatively, 80 percent of Rosenberg's puns have no basis in the original.

All this does not entirely invalidate Bloom's bold attempt to rescue the original J from twenty-five hundred years of overlaid editing and institutional interpretation, but it surely casts a large shadow of doubt on his undertaking. Bloom is an intuitive critic, something I happen to admire, but when he says that his "ear" tells him that this or that is J, that such was J's real intention, or that thus and so must have been the original J version displaced by those later dowdy establishment figures E and P, one is entitled to be skeptical. How can even the most brilliantly intuitive critic "hear" the nice inflections of an author's voice except in the author's own language? How seriously would we take someone who claimed that Shakespeare's sonnets were really written by a contemporary countess if we knew that the critic had read the sonnets mainly in a highly eccentric Italian translation, with intermittent references to the original aided by an English-Italian dictionary?

Bloom's attitude toward the idea that J was a woman is

a little slippery, perhaps appropriately so. He begins by announcing, quite sensibly, that "all our accounts of the Bible are scholarly fictions or religious fantasies, and generally serve rather tendentious purposes." His own undertaking then is presented as just such a fiction, one for which he offers an excellent justification. "When script becomes Scripture," he notes, "reading is numbed by taboo and inhibition. Even if imagining an author and calling her J is an arbitrary and personal fiction, something like that imagining is necessary if we are to be stirred out of our numbness." Fair enough, and the salutary effect of *The Book of J*, whatever its faults, is precisely that it has the power to stir us from the numbness of automatic response to a sacred text. Not surprisingly, however, as Bloom continues to expatiate on J, "she" more and more becomes a definite historical figure, not an arbitrary fiction, assigned a definite location in time, place, and social standing, which in turn is used to explain the intentions of her writing.

The decision about her gender, of which Bloom says he is intuitively convinced, is a fine way to *épater les fidèles*; every time the pronoun "she" occurs, readers are likely to find themselves shaken out of their preconceptions about the Bible, and that is all to the good. But the argument assumes a high degree of historical specificity (very much like that of Samuel Butler, who was persuaded, quite wrongly, that he had figured out precisely when and in what town of Sicily the authoress of the *Odyssey* lived, and what her age and personal condition were when she did the writing). J, then, was an aristocratic lady in the court of Rehoboam, a friendly competitor of the author of the David story, with whom she exchanged notes and rough drafts, and a passionate admirer of the figure of David, whom she represented obliquely in her Joseph.

Bloom may have taken heart in his project from Richard Friedman, whose *Who Wrote the Bible?* though more circumspect, seeks to pinpoint the temporal, geographical, and social location of each of the major biblical writers. One can admire the intellectual detective work of such undertakings, but given the paucity of reliable historical data we have, especially when anonymous authors who have been edited and combined with each other are involved, historical scholarship is bound to be more than halfway to historical fiction, as Bloom concedes at the beginning but almost forgets thereafter.

The difficulties of the task are twofold: dating texts that provide the scantest grounds for fixing them at any point in a span of two or three, sometimes four or more, centuries; and teasing out the original separate strands from the received text—the cunningly intertwined work of that genius or villain R, the Redactor (Friedman thinks he was Ezra the Scribe or someone close to Ezra). Perhaps the latter difficulty has been largely overcome by two centuries of text-critical scholarship, though I remain an agnostic about the certitude of identified textual components at a good many specific points, and biblical scholars have been quick to object that Bloom's J is full of mistaken attributions.

In this connection, every serious student of the Bible should look at Robert Polzin's *Samuel and the Deuteronomist.*[3] With a massive apparatus of notes and the most detailed reference to previous scholarship, Polzin contends that the neat divisions of the text of Samuel into Deuteronomistic Framework, Ark Narrative, Succession History, and so forth, become unconvincing in the face of the architectonic literary character of the text. Some of Polzin's arguments for artful unity by way of foreshadowing and allegorization within the narrative of subsequent themes may be too ingenious, but he does put forth a powerful, meticulously documented reading that makes one think twice about the atomistic conclusions of modern biblical scholarship.

But even if we assume that we know confidently in all significant instances what is J, E, and P, there remains the intractable problem of what Sir Edmund Leach has called "unscrambling the omelette." Perhaps there once was a splendid J narrative from Adam to Moses, but all that is left of it is what R decided to splice with E and P. The J texts that have come down to us, even if they had a much better translator than David Rosenberg, are an intermittent, inadequate story, a poor thing compared to the wonderful orchestration that R has made of all his sources and that we are accustomed to read. Richard Friedman aptly concludes his excavative quest for individual authors with a chapter devoted to the splendid complexities and play of tensions of the final synthesis, a whole that he readily declares is greater than the sum of its parts. Bloom, by contrast, is mesmerized by the idea of the individual author of genius, and so for him whatever subsequent tradition did with J emasculates, or rather, defeminizes her unique imaginative authority.

In any case, unscrambling the omelette is actually less insuperable a difficulty than figuring out when the original eggs were laid, and by which hens. Bloom invests more than is prudent in the idea that J flourished in the court of Rehoboam, Solomon's son, in the latter part of the tenth century B.C.E. The evidence that the Pentateuch addresses the politics of the Davidic dynasty right after the split of the monarchy into two kingdoms is, to put it mildly, highly inferential. Bloom latches onto Richard Friedman's suggestion that J refers in code several times to Rehoboam by using the word *raḥav*, "broad," from which that king's name is derived. (The word does not occur in E.) But since this is a perfectly common Hebrew adjective, the line of reasoning resembles that of an analyst in some remote future who, looking at English texts of our own period, would locate them in England between 1939 and 1945 because several occurrences of *church* were seized on as veiled allusions to Churchill.

Bloom repeatedly relies on the notion that J and the author of the David narrative knew each other personally and undertook parallel literary enterprises focusing on different historical settings. It is a reasonable enough guess that the David author (I happen to think there was one, not several) lived in Jerusalem two or three generations after David, so the proposed location in the court of Rehoboam may not be far from the mark. But was J his contemporary? There is actually a good deal of evidence in 1 and 2 Samuel, as there is in Joshua and Judges, that J's writing was already a publicly known text, familiar in minute detail, which could be mined for literary allusions. This would obviously not be the case if the narrative of J existed for the David author merely as a friend's work in progress, according to Bloom's own fiction.

Let me rapidly review one example I discussed at length elsewhere (see pages 114-17). When David's son Amnon is about to rape his half sister Tamar (2 Samuel 13), he clears the room with the words *hotsi'u khol 'ish me`alai*, literally, "Take everyone out from before me," the selfsame words Joseph uses before he reveals his identity to his brothers. Then he has only the most brutally abrupt words of dialogue to pronounce to Tamar, "Lie with me, my sister," the very same words, with a shift from masculine imperative to feminine imperative, and the addition of the marker of incest, "my sister," that Potiphar's wife uses as she prepares to lay lustful hands on Joseph. In each case, the verbal response of the intended victim of sexual assault is a breathless verbosity that stands in dramatic contrast to the blunt conciseness of the assailant. Finally, after the rape, we are told that Tamar has been wearing a *ketonet pasim*, an ornamented tunic or "coat of many colors." Joseph is the only other figure in the whole Bible who is said to wear that garment. Her tunic, like his, may well be bloodied after an act of fraternal violence, since she is a virgin rape victim.

What we have, then, in 2 Samuel 13, is a brilliantly interwoven thread of allusions to the Joseph story *in J's textual version*, shrewdly set in reverse chronological order. The climax of the Joseph story, the self-revelation and the reconciliation with the brothers—"take everyone out from before me"—is here the starting point, a prelude to an act of violence of brother against sister, which will entail fatal consequences. Then the echo of the failed sexual attempt on Joseph in the successful sexual assault on Tamar pointedly stresses the crucial difference in physical vulnerability between male and female: Joseph is able to break away and run outside; Tamar is overpowered, a fact the narrator underscores by choosing three verbs indicating superior strength to represent Amnon's act. Finally, the ornamented tunic that is the beginning of Joseph's disaster at the hands of his brothers and a key element in his whole plot, the token of his seeming death, is introduced at the end of Tamar's story as an emblem of the personal catastrophe and social disgrace she has suffered.

Even in this quick summary of the evidence, it should be apparent that the author of 2 Samuel 13 could have cast such a cunning network of significant allusions only if both he and his audience were quite familiar with J's Joseph story in a version verbally very close to the one that has come down to us. This would place J at the very least a couple of generations before the David writer.

It is certainly to Bloom's credit as a literary theorist that through two decades during which Roland Barthes's idea of the "death of the author" has reigned supreme, when critics became accustomed to speak of "the text" doing things rather than the writer, he has remained resolutely attached to the idea of individual personalities willfully asserting themselves in the act of writing, struggling with other personalities who are their predecessors. J, along with Shakespeare, to whom he often compares her, is his parade example of the "strong writer," one of the two strongest in our whole tradition; after her, all subsequent writers find themselves "belated," wrestling in vain to match her achievement.

Since, as we have seen, the fixing of temporal priority among biblical writers is by no means simple, it is instructive to note that a new book, working on avowedly Bloomian assumptions, by Leslie Brisman, a Yale colleague and friend of Bloom's, uses those assumptions to arrive at precisely the opposite conclusion.[4] In Brisman's ingenious, resourceful reading, J is a belated writer confronted by the deft but orthodox version of the great story of origins already established by E. In this view, J is also seen as a canny, daring, surprising writer, but he (not she, here) repeatedly uses those resources to put a new spin on E, to introduce ironies and ambiguities into E's received version. Perhaps this is a little improbable, but, then again, why not? Or why not J and E as contemporaries, as Richard Friedman suggests, the former working in the Southern Kingdom, the latter in the Northern one?

The issue of gender, though constantly flaunted by Bloom, is in the end much less important for him than the notion of J as the ultimate "strong writer." It must be said that the evidence offered for J's female identity is rather tenuous. We are repeatedly told, often with engaging wit, that J in Genesis exercises an extraordinary degree of imaginative sympathy for the plight of women and the viewpoint of the female characters. But this is also true of the authors of Judges and Samuel—note the instance of the rape of Tamar—not to speak of later books like Ruth and Esther. By the same reasoning, which Samuel Butler similarly invokes for the *Odyssey*, one could easily conclude that *Anna Karenina*, with its splendidly realized if doomed heroine and its large gallery of repulsive, feckless, or clumsy men, must have been written by a woman. The evidence of literary history suggests that there is no reason at all to assume that literary imaginations of the first order are trapped in this fashion within the walls of gender.

Bloom goes further in his feminizing view of J, contending that she "had no heroes, only heroines." I am not sure one should so readily dismiss Jacob as a hero simply because, like Odysseus, he is wily and works himself into ambiguous situations, and Bloom is compelled to exclude the major example of Joseph by claiming that J's only ideal male figure was David, and Joseph was put forth as a "surrogate" for David. In point of fact, the earliest stratum of literary narrative drawn on by J may have been prior to David. What is clear is that the author of the David story in our received text made explicit verbal allusions to J's version of both Joseph and Jacob.

The ultimate problem about Bloom's effort "to seek a reversal of twenty-five hundred years of institutionalized misreading" is not just the paucity and the elusiveness of the literary-historical data but the discrepancy between his conception of authorship, essentially based on Blake's struggle to overcome Milton, and the nature of the ancient texts. For all its startling originality, the Bible as the work of anonymous writers is a strongly traditional form of literary expression in which, for example, even the keenest analysts have difficulty in distinguishing between the style of J and E except on limited terminological grounds. (Samuel Butler made a fundamental mistake analogous to Bloom's in assuming a definite biography for his authoress, not guessing the Greek epic's oral-formulaic composition with traditional materials that would be discovered several decades later.) The Documentary Hypothesis is quite properly designated as such, and not as an Authorial Hypothesis. It is generally thought that the Priestly Document, P, is the product of a school of writers, or perhaps the accretion of successive generations of writers. There is no compelling reason to assume that J or E is the unitary work of a single man or woman.

To cite one small instance, Bloom has a good deal to say about J's cryptic Bridegroom of Blood story in Exodus 4 as a characteristic expression of her imaginative daring. For him, the strange tale of God's attempt on Moses' life is of a piece with J's sophisticated feminine attitude toward the Deity in general, which he describes as "a mother's somewhat wary but still proudly amused stance toward a favorite son who has grown up to be benignly powerful but also eccentrically irascible." What this ignores, in regard to both the style and the substance of the episode, is its manifestly archaic character. The consensus of biblical scholarship, with which for once I emphatically concur, sees the Bridegroom of Blood as very old, mythic material, embedded, for reasons we cannot know, in the literary tradition that eventuated in J. It strains credence to imagine that the writer responsible for the psychological probing, the rich comedy, and the stylistic elegance of J's Joseph was also the "sensibility" that produced the Bridegroom of Blood. For the fundamentalism of revealed faith Bloom substitutes a fundamentalism of authorial personality, and I cannot believe that brings us close to the distinctive literary nature of the ancient Hebrew texts.

In regard, then, to the character of the writer, his or her gender and historical setting, *The Book of J* is indeed a fiction or fantasy, and not necessarily a helpful one. There remains to be said a final word or two about Bloom's larger project. As I have already indicated, by dint of sheer imaginative energy, a willingness to look at the antithetical hidden side of things, he does succeed in opening up a new vista on this text that has determined so much of our culture. His chief contribution is to peel back the thick, multilayered film of religious interpretation and allow us to contemplate the possibility that the earliest major author of the Bible was not really a religious writer, at least not in any sense assimilable to our concepts of religion. "The distinction between sacred and secular texts," he says at the outset, "results from social and political decisions, and thus is not a literary distinction at all." He encourages us to see J as a writer continuously delighting in the very possibilities of representing human and divine realities, "uncanny, tricky, sublime, ironic, a visionary of incommensurates, and so the direct ancestor of Kafka." J "overwhelms" us, in the Bloomian terminology of strong writing, by determining the very conditions through which the psychology of men and women might be represented in literature. After J, only Shakespeare again "changed us by changing representation itself."

In one respect, even Shakespeare does not match J, for she had the imaginative boldness to conceive God himself as a complex literary character—a conception that even recent literary analysis has rarely been able to assimilate, because we remain in thrall to later, theological imaginings of a transcendent God who exists beyond the realm of mere literature. Such notions of what Bloom wryly calls a "divine bureaucrat" have little to do with the boldness of J's imaginative world. Commenting on ancient Hebrew anthropomorphism, Bloom observes that "the normative and the scholarly are crude, while J is sophisticated. Her idea of Yahweh is imaginative, even Shakespearian, while the normative reductions of her Yahweh are quite primitive."

Looking back over Bloom's many books, one detects in him a hidden aspiration to move from the role of critic to that of heresiarch, to become the pathfinder of a Jewish way— alternately literary and gnostic—antithetical to received religion. In his attempted recovery of J, he has found at the very source of Jewish tradition a figure who articulates a "monistic vitalism" beyond all institutional categories, beyond the neat division of the world into banned and blessed. There are gaping holes in the fabric of his argument, but that does not necessarily mean we should decline his invitation to look at the ancient writings with fresh eyes.

CHAPTER 8

The Medium of
Poetry

Exactly what is the poetry of the Bible, and what role
does it play in giving form to the biblical religious vision? The
second of these two questions obviously involves all sorts of
imponderables. One would think that, by contrast, the first
question should have a straightforward answer; but in fact
there has been considerable confusion through the ages about
where there is poetry in the Bible and about the principles on
which that poetry works.

To begin with, biblical poetry occurs almost exclusively in
the Hebrew Bible. There are, of course, grandly poetic passages in the New Testament—perhaps most impressively in
the Apocalypse—but only the Magnificat of Luke 1 is fashioned as formal verse. Readers of the Old Testament often
cannot easily see where the poetry is supposed to be, because
in the King James Version, which has been the text used by

most English-speaking people, nothing is laid out as lines of verse. This confusing typographic procedure is in turn faithful to the Hebrew manuscript tradition, which runs everything together in dense, unpunctuated columns. (There are just a few exceptions where there is spacing out roughly corresponding to lines of verse, as in the Song of the Sea, Exodus 15; in Moses' valedictory song, Deuteronomy 32; and in an occasional manuscript of Psalms.)

This graphic leveling of poetry with prose in the text has been accompanied by a kind of cultural amnesia about biblical poetics. Over the centuries, Psalms was most clearly perceived as poetry, probably because of the actual musical indications in the texts and the obvious liturgical function of many of the poems. The status as poetry of the Song of Songs and of Job was, because of the lyric beauty of the one and the grandeur of the other, also generally kept in sight, however farfetched the notions about the formal character of the verse in these books. Proverbs was somewhat more intermittently seen as poetry, and it was often not understood that the Prophets cast the larger part of their message in verse. Finally, it is only in our century that scholars have begun to realize to what extent the prose narratives of the Bible are studded with brief verse insets, usually introduced at dramatically justified or otherwise significant junctures in the stories.

Over the last two millennia—and, for many, down to the present—being a reader of biblical poetry has been like being a reader of Dryden and Pope who comes from a culture with no concept of rhyme: you would loosely grasp that the language was intricately organized as verse, but with the uneasy feeling that you were somehow missing something essential you could not quite define. The central informing convention of biblical verse was rediscovered in the mideighteenth century by a scholarly Anglican bishop, Robert Lowth. He proposed that lines of biblical verse comprised two or three "members" (which I shall call "versets") parallel to each other in meaning.

Like many a good discovery, Bishop Lowth's perception has not fared as well as it might have. The realization soon dawned that some of what he called parallelism was not semantically parallel at all. This recognition led to a sometimes confusing proliferation of subcategories of parallelism and, in our own time, to various baby-with-bathwater operations in which syllable count, units of syntax, or some other formal feature was proposed as the basis for biblical poetry, parallelism being relegated to a secondary or incidental position. In another direction, at least one scholar, despairing of a coherent account of biblical verse, has contended that there was no distinct concept of formal versification in ancient Israel but merely a "continuum" of parallelistic rhetoric from prose to what we misleadingly call poetry.[1] Some of these confusions can be sorted out, and as a result we may be able to see more clearly the distinctive strength and beauty of the biblical poems, for an understanding of the poetic system is always a precondition to reading the poem well.

Semantic parallelism, though by no means invariably present, is a prevalent feature of biblical verse. That is, if the poet says "hearken" in the first verset, he is apt to say something like "listen" or "heed" in the second verset. This parallelism of meaning, which is often joined with a balancing of the number of rhythmic stresses between the versets and sometimes by parallel syntactic patterns as well,[2] seems to have played a role roughly analogous to that of iambic pentameter in Shakespeare's dramatic verse: it is an underlying formal model that the poet feels free to modify or occasionally to abandon altogether. In longer biblical poems, a departure from parallelism is sometimes used to mark the end of a distinct segment; elsewhere parallelism is now and again set aside in favor of a small-scale narrative sequence within the line; and a few poets appear simply to have been less fond than others of the symmetries of parallelism.

Before attempting to sharpen this rather general concept of poetic parallelism, let me offer some brief examples of its basic patterns of development. David's victory psalm (2 Samuel 22) presents a nice variety of possibilities because it is relatively long for a biblical poem and includes quasi-narrative elements and discrete segments with formally marked transitions. Few of its fifty-three lines of verse approach a perfect coordinated parallelism not only of meaning but also of syntax and rhythmic stresses. Thus: "For with you I charge a barrier, / with my God I vault a wall" (verse 30). Here each semantically parallel term in the two versets is in the same syntactic position: with you / with my God, I charge / I vault, a barrier / a wall. Although our knowledge of the phonetics of biblical Hebrew involves a certain margin of conjecture, the line with its system of stresses, as vocalized in the Masoretic Hebrew text, would sound something like this: *ki bekhá 'arúts gedúd / belohái adáleg-shúr*, yielding a 3 + 3 parallelism of stressed syllables, which in fact is the most common pattern in biblical verse. (The rule is that there are never fewer than two stresses in a verset and never more than four, and no two stresses follow each other without an intervening unstressed syllable; and there are often asymmetrical combinations of 4 + 3 or 3 + 2.)

It is hardly surprising that biblical poets should very often seek to avoid such regularity as we have just seen, through different kinds of elegant—and sometimes significant—variation. Frequently, syntactically disparate clauses are used to convey a parallelism of meaning, as in verse 29: "For you are my lamp, O Lord, / the Lord lights up my darkness," where the second-person predicative assertion that the Lord is a lamp is transformed into a third-person narrative statement in which the Lord now governs a verb of illumination. Even when the syntax of the two versets is much closer than this, variations may be introduced, as in two lines from the beginning of the poem (verses 5–6) that describe the speaker as having been on the brink of death. I will reproduce the precise word order of the Hebrew, though at the cost of awkwardness, for biblical Hebrew usage is much more flexible than modern English in regard to subject-predicate order.

> *For there encompassed me the breakers of death,*
>   *the rivers of destruction terrified me.*
> *The cords of Sheol surrounded me,*
>   *there greeted me the snares of death.*

The syntactic shape of these two lines, which preserve a regular semantic parallelism through all four versets as well as a 3–3 stress in both lines, is a double chiasm: (1) encompassed-breakers-rivers-terrified; (2) cords-surrounded-greeted-snares. In the first line the verbs of surrounding are the outside terms, the entrapping agencies of death, the inside terms of the chiasm (abba); and in the second line this order is reversed (baab). This maneuver, which, like the interlinear parallelism, is quite common in biblical verse, may be nothing more than elegant variation to avoid mechanical repetitiousness, though one suspects here that the chiastic boxing in and the reversal of terms help reinforce the feeling of entrapment that is being expressed: as the two lines unfold, the reader can scarcely choose between a sense of being multifariously surrounded and a sense of the multiplicity of the instruments of death.

Another frequent pattern for bracketing the two versets together involves an elliptical syntactic parallelism, usually through the introduction of a verb at the beginning of the first verset that does double duty for the second verset as well, as in verse 15: "He sent forth bolts and scattered them, / lightning, and overwhelmed them." The ellipsis of "he-sent-forth" (one word and one accented syllable in the Hebrew) produces a 3–2 stress pattern, which also involves a counterposing of three Hebrew words to two. (Biblical Hebrew is much more compact than any translation can suggest, with subject, object, possessive pronoun, preposition, and so forth indicated by suffix or prefix; and most words have only one accent.) This rhythmic truncation of the second verset conveys a certain abruptness that the poet may have felt intuitively to be appropriate for the violent action depicted.

Elsewhere in biblical poetry, when ellipsis through a double-duty verb occurs while the parallelism of stresses between versets is maintained, the extra rhythmic unit in the second verset is used to develop semantic material introduced in the first verset. Here is a characteristic instance from Moses' valedictory song (Deut. 32:13): "He suckled him with honey from a rock, / and oil from a flinty stone." That is, since the verb *he-suckled-him-with* (again a single word in the Hebrew) does double duty for the second verset, rhythmic space is freed in the second half of the line in which the poet can elaborate the simple general term *rock* into the complex term *flinty stone*, which is a particular instance of the general category, and one that brings out the quality of hardness. (I shall discuss in detail later the development of meaning within semantic parallelism.)

It is beyond my purposes here to classify all the subcategories of parallelism that present themselves in David's victory psalm, but two additional cases are worth looking at to round out our provisional sense of the spectrum of possibilities. Verse 9, like the one that precedes it in 2 Samuel 22, is triadic: "Smoke came out of his nostrils, / fire from his mouth consumed, / coals glowed round him." First, let me comment briefly on the role of triadic lines in the biblical poetic system. Dyadic lines, as in all our previous examples, definitely predominate, but the poets have free recourse to triadic lines, with none of the uneasy conscience manifested, say, by English Augustan poets when they introduce triplets into a poem composed in heroic couplets. In longer poems such as this, triadic lines can be used to mark the beginning or the end of a segment, as here the triadic verses 8–9 initiate the awesome seismic description of the Lord descending from on high to do battle with his foes. Elsewhere, triadic lines are simply interspersed with dyadic ones, and in some poems they are cultivated when the poet wants to express a sense of tension or instability, using the third verset to contrast or even to reverse the first two parallel versets. Now, the smoke-fire-coals series quoted above involves approximately parallel concepts and actions, but the terms are also *sequenced*, temporarily and logically, moving from smoke to its source to an incandescence so intense that everything around it is ignited. This progression, too, reflects a more general feature of poetic parallelism in the Bible to which we shall return.

Finally, biblical poetry abounds in lines like the one immediately following the line just quoted: "He tilted the heavens, came down, / deep mist beneath his feet" (verse 10). Here the only "parallelism" between the second verset and the first is one of rhythmic stresses (again 3–3). Otherwise, the second verset differs from the first in both syntax and meaning. The fairly frequent occurrence of such lines is no reason either to contort our definition of parallelism or to throw out the concept as a governing principle of Hebrew verse. The system, as I proposed before, is rather one in which semantic parallelism predominates without having to be regarded as an absolute necessity for every line. In this instance the poet seems to be pursuing a visual realization of the narrative momentum of the line (and, indeed, the momentum carries down through a whole sequence of lines); first he presents the Lord tilting the heavens and descending and then, as the eye of the beholder plunges, a picture in the locative second clause of the deep mist beneath God's feet as he descends. This yields a more striking effect than would a regular parallelism such as "He tilted the heavens, came down, / he plummeted to the earth," and is a small but characteristic indication of the suppleness with which the general convention of parallelism is put to use by biblical poets.

Now, the greatest stumbling block in approaching biblical poetry has been the misconception that parallelism implies synonymity, saying the same thing twice in different words. I would argue that good poetry at all times is an intellectually robust activity to which such laziness is alien, that poets understand more subtly than linguists that there are no true synonyms, and that the ancient Hebrew poets are constantly advancing their meanings where the casual ear catches mere repetition. Not surprisingly, some lines of biblical poetry approach a condition of equivalent statement between the versets more than others do. Thus: "He preserves the paths of justice, / and the way of his faithful ones he guards" (Prov. 2:8). By my count, however, such instances of nearly synonymous restatement occur in less than a quarter of the lines of verse in the biblical corpus.

The dominant pattern is a focusing, heightening, or specification of ideas, images, actions, and themes from one verset to the next. If something is broken in the first verset, it is smashed or shattered in the second verset; if a city is destroyed in the first verset, it is turned into a heap of rubble in the second. A general term in the first half of the line is typically followed by a specific instance of the general category in the second half; or, again, a literal statement in the first verse becomes a metaphor or hyperbole in the second. The notion that repetition in a text is very rarely simple restatement has long been understood by rhetoricians and literary theorists. Thus, the Elizabethan rhetorician Hoskins—might the King James translators have read him?—acutely observes that "in speech there is no repetition without importance."[3] What this means to us as readers of biblical poetry is that instead of listening to an imagined drumbeat of repetitions, we need constantly to look for something new happening from one part of the line to the next.

The case of numbers in parallelism is especially instructive. If the underlying principle were really synonymity, we would expect to find, say, "forty" in one verset and "two score" in the other. In fact, the almost invariable rule is an ascent on the numerical scale from first to second verset, either by one, or by a decimal multiple, or by a decimal multiple of the first number added to itself. And as with numbers, so with images and ideas; there is a steady amplification or intensification of the original terms.

Here is a paradigmatic numerical instance: "How could one pursue a thousand, / and two put ten thousand to flight?" (Deut. 32:30). An amusing illustration of scholarly misconception about what is involved poetically in such cases is a common contemporary view of the triumphal song chanted by the Israelite women: "Saul has smitten his thousands, / David, his tens of thousands" (1 Sam. 18:7). It has been suggested that Saul's anger over these words reflects his paranoia, for he should have realized that in poetry it is a formulaic necessity to move from a thousand to ten thousand, and so the women really intended no slight to him.[4] Such a suggestion assumes that somehow poetry conjures with formulaic devices indifferent to meaning. Saul may indeed have been paranoid, but he knew perfectly well how the Hebrew poetry of his era worked and understood that meanings were quite pointedly developed from one half of the line to the other. In fact, the prose narrative in 1 Samuel 18 strongly confirms the rightness of Saul's "reading," for the people are clearly said to be extravagantly enamored of David and not at all of Saul.

Let me propose a few examples of this dynamic movement within the line, and then try to suggest something about the compelling religious and visionary ends served by this distinctive poetics. (For the sake of convenience, I have chosen almost all my examples from Psalms.) In the first group, the italics in the second versets indicate the point at which seeming repetition becomes a focusing, a heightening, or a concretization of the original material: "Let me hear joy and gladness, / let *the bones you have crushed exult*" (Ps. 51:10); "How long, O Lord, will you be perpetually incensed, / *like a flame* your wrath *will burn*" (Ps. 79:5); "He counts the number of the stars, / each one he *calls by name*" (Ps. 147:4).

These three lines illustrate a small spectrum of possibilities of semantic focusing between the two versets. In the first example, the general joy and gladness of the first versets become sharper through the contrastive introduction of the crushed bones in the second verset, and bones exulting is, of course, a more vividly metaphorical restatement of the idea of rejoicing. In the second example, the possible hint of the notion of heat in the term for "incensed" (*te'enaf*, which might derive etymologically from the hot breath from the nostrils) becomes in the second verset a full-fledged metaphor of wrath burning like a flame. In the third example, there is no recourse to metaphor, but there is an obvious focusing in the "parallel" verbs of the two versets: calling something by name, which in the biblical world implies intimate relation, knowledge of the essence of the thing, is a good deal more than mere counting. The logical structure of this line, which is quite typical of biblical poetics, would be something like this: not only can God count the innumerable stars (first verset), but he even knows the name of (or gives a name to) each single star.

Since the three examples we have just considered move from incipiently metaphorical to explicitly metaphorical to literal, a few brief observations may be in order about the role of figurative language in biblical poetics. Striking imagery does not seem to have been especially valued for itself, as it would come to be in many varieties of European post-Romantic poetry. Some poets favor nonfigurative language, and very often, as we have seen, figures are introduced in the second verset as a convenient means among several possible ones for heightening some notion that appears in the first verset. In any case, the biblical poets on the whole were inclined to draw on a body of more or less familiar images without consciously striving for originality of invention in their imagery. Wrath kindles, burns, consumes; protection is a canopy, a sheltering wing, shade in blistering heat; solace or renewal is dew, rain, streams of fresh water, and so forth. The effectiveness of the image derives in part from its very familiarity, perhaps its archetypal character, in part from the way it is placed in context and, quite often, extended and intensified by elaboration through several lines or by reinforcement with related images.

However, there is no overarching symbolic pattern, as some have claimed, in the images used by biblical poets, and no conventional limitation is set on the semantic fields from which the images are drawn. Though biblical poetry abounds in pastoral, agricultural, topographical, and meteorological images, the manufacturing processes of ancient Near Eastern urban culture are also frequently enlisted by the poets: the crafts of the weaver, the dyer, the launderer, the potter, the builder, the smith, and so forth. This freedom to draw images from all areas of experience, even in a poetic corpus largely committed to conventional figures, allows for some striking individual images. The Job poet in particular excels in such invention, likening the swiftness of human existence to the movement of the shuttle on a loom, the fashioning of the child in the womb to the curdling of cheese, the mists over the waters of creation to swaddling clothes, and in general making his imagery a strong correlative of his extraordinary sense both of man's creaturely contingency and of God's overwhelming power.

As for the operation of poetic parallelism within the line, the possibilities of complication of meaning are too various to be discussed comprehensively here, but an important second category of development between versets deserves mention. In the following pair of lines, the parallelism within the line is of a rather special kind, involving something other than intensification:

> *The teaching of his God is in his heart,*
> *his footsteps will not stumble.*
> *The wicked spies out the just,*
> *and seeks to kill him. (Ps. 37:31–32)*

In the first of these lines, the statements of the two versets do correspond to each other, but the essential nature of the correspondence is *causal:* if you keep the Lord's teaching, you can count on avoiding calamity. In the next line, causation is allied with temporal sequence. That is, to try to kill someone is a more extreme act of malice than to lie in wait for him and hence an "intensification," but the two are different points in a miniature narrative continuum: first the lying in wait, then the attempt to kill. We see the same pattern in the following image of destruction, where the first verset presents the breaking down of fortress walls, and the second verset the destruction of the fortress itself: "You burst through all his barriers, / you turned his strongholds to rubble" (Ps. 89:41).

It is sometimes asked what happened to narrative verse in ancient Israel, for whereas the principal narratives of most other ancient cultures are in poetry, narrative proper in the Hebrew Bible is almost exclusively reserved for prose. One partial answer is that the narrative impulse, which for a variety of reasons is withdrawn from the larger structure of the poem, often reappears on a more microscopic level, within the line, or in a brief sequence of lines, in the articulation of the poem's imagery, as in the examples just cited. In quite a few instances this narrativity within the line is perfectly congruent with what I have described as the parallelism of intensification. Both elements are beautifully transparent in these two versets from Isaiah: "Like a pregnant woman whose time draws near, / she trembles, she screams in her birth pangs" (Is. 26:17). The second verset of course, not only is more concretely focused than the first but also represents a later moment in the same process—from very late pregnancy to the midst of labor.

This impulse of compact narrativity within the line is so common that it is often detectable even in the one-line poems that are introduced as dramatic heightening in the prose narratives. Thus, when Jacob sees Joseph's bloodied tunic and concludes that his son has been killed, he follows the words of pained recognition, "It's my son's tunic," with a line of verse that is a kind of miniature elegy: "An evil beast has devoured him, / torn, oh torn, is Joseph" (Gen. 37:33). The second verset is at once a focusing of the act of devouring and an incipiently narrative transition from the act to its awful consequence: a ravening beast has devoured him, and as the concrete result his body has been torn to shreds.

We see another variation of the underlying pattern in the line of quasi-prophetic (and quite mistaken) rebuke that the priest Eli pronounces to the distraught Hannah, whose lips have been moving in silent prayer: "How long will you be drunk? / Put away your wine!" (1 Sam. 1:14). Some analysts might be tempted to claim that the two versets here, despite their semantic and syntactic dissimilarity, have the same "deep structure" because they both express outrage at

Hannah's supposed state of drunkenness, but I think we are in fact meant to read the line by noting differentiation. The first verset suggests that to continue in a state of inebriation in the sanctuary is intolerable; the second verset projects that attitude forward on a temporal axis (narrativity in the imperative mode) by drawing the consequence that the woman addressed must sober up at once.

Beyond the scale of the one-line poem, this element of narrativity between versets plays an important role in the development of meaning because so many biblical poems, even if they are not explicitly narrative, are concerned in one way or another with process. Psalm 102 is an instructive case in point. The poem is a collective supplication on behalf of Israel in captivity. (Since it begins and ends in the first-person singular, it is conceivable that it is a reworking of an older individual supplication.) A good many lines exhibit the movement of intensification or focusing that we observed earlier. Verse 3 is a good example: "For my days have gone up in smoke, / my bones are charred like a hearth." Other lines reflect complementarity, such as verse 6: "I resembled the great owl of the desert, / I became like an owl among ruins." But because the speaker of the poem is, after all, trying to project a possibility of change out of the wasteland of exile in which he finds himself, a number of lines show a narrative progression from the first verset to the second since *something is happening*, and it is not just a static condition that is being reported.

Narrativity is felt particularly as God moves into action in history: "For the Lord has built up Zion, / he appears in his glory" (verse 16). That is, as a consequence of his momentous act of rebuilding the ruins of Zion (first verset), the glory of the Lord again becomes globally visible (second verset). Then the Lord looks down from heaven "to listen to the groans of the captive, / to free those condemned to death" (verse 20)—first the listening, then the act of liberation. God's praise thus emanates from the rebuilt Jerusalem to which the exiles return "when nations gather together, / and kingdoms, to serve the Lord" (verse 22). Elsewhere in Psalms, the gathering together of nations and kingdoms may suggest a mustering of armies for attack on Israel, but the last phrase of the line, "to serve [or worship] the Lord," functions as a climactic narrative revelation: this assembly of nations is to worship God in his mountain sanctuary, now splendidly reestablished. In sum, the narrative momentum of these individual lines picks up a sense of historical process and helps align the collective supplication with the prophecies of return to Zion in Deutero-Isaiah, with which this poem is probably contemporaneous.

This last point may begin to suggest to the ordinary reader, who with good reason thinks of the Bible primarily as a corpus of religious writings, what all these considerations of formal poetics have to do with the urgent spiritual concerns of the ancient Hebrew poets. I do not think there is ever a one-to-one correspondence between poetic systems and views of reality, but a particular poetics may encourage or reinforce a particular orientation toward reality. For all the untold reams of commentary on the Bible, this remains a sadly neglected question. One symptomatic case in point: a standard work on the basic forms of prophetic discourse by the German scholar Claus Westermann never once mentions the poetic vehicle used by the Prophets and makes no formal distinction between, say, a short prophetic statement in prose by Elijah and a complex poem by Isaiah.[5] Any intrinsic connection between the kind of poetry the Prophets spoke and the nature of their message is simply never contemplated.

Biblical poetry, as I have tried to show, is characterized by an intensifying or narrative development within the line; and quite often this "horizontal" movement is then projected downward in a "vertical" focusing movement through a sequence of lines or even through a whole poem. This means that the poetry of the Bible is concerned above all with dynamic process moving toward some culmination. The two most common structures, then, of biblical poetry are a movement of intensification of images, concepts, and themes through a sequence of lines, and a narrative movement—which most often pertains to the development of metaphorical acts but can also refer to literal events, as in much prophetic poetry. The account of the creation in the first chapter of Genesis might serve as a model for the conception of reality that underlies most of this body of poetry: from day to day new elements are added in a continuous process that culminates in the seventh day, the primordial Sabbath. It would require a close reading of whole poems to see fully how this model is variously manifested in the different genres of biblical poetry, but I can at least sketch out the ways in which the model is perceptible in verse addressed to personal, philosophical, and historical issues.

The poetry of Psalms has evinced an extraordinary power to speak to the lives of countless individual readers and has echoed through the work of writers as different as Augustine, George Herbert, Paul Claudel, and Dylan Thomas. Some of the power of the Psalms may be attributed to their being such effective "devotions upon emergent occasions," as John Donne, another poet strongly moved by these biblical poems, called a collection of his meditations. The sense of emergency virtually defines the numerically predominant subgenre of psalm, the supplication. The typical—though not invariable—movement of the supplication is a rising line of intensity toward a climax of terror or desperation. The paradigmatic supplication would sound something like this: you have forgotten me, O Lord; you have hidden your face from me; you have thrown me to the mercies of my enemies; I totter on the brink of death, plunge into the darkness of the Pit. At this intolerable point of culmination, when there is nothing left for the speaker but the terrible contemplation of his own imminent extinction, a sharp reversal takes place. The speaker either prays to God to draw him out of the abyss or, in some poems, confidently asserts that God is in fact already working this wondrous rescue. It is clear why these poems have reverberated so strongly in the moments of crisis, spiritual or physical, of so many readers, and I would suggest that the distinctive capacity of biblical poetics to advance along a steeply inclined plane of mounting intensities does much to help the poets imaginatively realize both the experience of crisis and the dramatic reversal at the end.

Certainly there are other, less dynamic varieties of poetic structure represented in the biblical corpus, including the Book of Psalms. The general fondness of ancient Hebrew writers in all genres for so-called envelope structures (in which the conclusion somehow echoes terms or whole phrases from the beginning) leads in some poems to balanced, symmetrically enclosed forms, occasionally even to a division into parallel strophes, as in the Song of the Sea (Exodus 15). The neatest paradigm for such symmetrical structures is Psalm 8, which, articulating a firm belief in the beautiful hierarchical perfection of creation, opens and closes with the refrain "Lord, our master, / how majestic is your name in all the earth!"

Symmetrical structures, because they tend to imply a confident sense of the possibility of encapsulating perception, are favored in particular by poets in the main line of Hebrew Wisdom literature—but not by the Job poet, who works in what has been described as the "radical wing" of biblical Wisdom writing. Thus, the separate poems that constitute Chapters 5 and 7 of Proverbs, though the former uses narrative elements and the latter is a freestanding narrative, equally employ neat envelope structures as frames to emphasize their didactic points. The Hymn to Wisdom in Job 28, which most scholars consider to be an interpolation, stands out from the surrounding poetry not only in its assured tone but also in its structure, being neatly divided into three symmetrical strophes marked by a refrain. Such instances, however, are no more than exceptions that prove the rule, for the structure that predominates in all genres of biblical poetry is one in which a kind of semantic pressure is built from verset to verset and line to line, finally reaching a climax or a climax and reversal.

This momentum of intensification is felt somewhat differently in the text that is in many respects the most astonishing poetic achievement in the biblical corpus, the Book of Job. Whereas the psalm poets provided voices for the anguish and exultation of real people, Job is a fictional character, as the folktale stylization of the introductory prose narrative means to intimate. In the rounds of debate with the three Friends, poetry spoken by fictional figures is used to ponder the enigma of arbitrary suffering that seems a constant element of the human condition. One of the ways in which we are invited to gauge the difference between the Friends and Job is through the different kinds of poetry they utter—the Friends stringing together beautifully polished clichés (sometimes virtually a parody of the poetry of Proverbs and Psalms), Job making constant disruptive departures in the images he uses, in the extraordinary muscularity of his language line after line. The poetry Job speaks is an instrument forged to sound the uttermost depths of suffering, and so he adopts movements of intensification to focus in on his anguish. The intolerable point of culmination is followed not, as in Psalms, by a confident prayer for salvation but by a death wish, whose only imagined relief is the extinction of life and mind, or by a kind of desperate shriek of outrage to the Lord.

When God finally answers Job out of the whirlwind, he responds with an order of poetry formally allied to Job's own remarkable poetry, but larger in scope and greater in power (from the compositional viewpoint, it is the sort of risk only a writer of genius could take and get away with). That is, God picks up many of Job's key images, especially from the death-wish poem with which Job began (Chapter 3), and his discourse is shaped by a powerful movement of intensification, coupled with an implicitly narrative sweep from the creation to the play of natural forces to the teeming world of animal life. But whereas Job's intensities are centripetal and necessarily egocentric, God's intensities carry us back and forth through the pulsating vital movements of the whole created world. The culmination of the poem God speaks is not a cry of self or a dream of self snuffed out but the terrible beauty of the Leviathan, on the uncanny borderline between zoology and mythology, where what is fierce and strange, beyond the ken and conquest of man, is the climactic manifestation of a splendidly providential creation that merely anthropomorphic notions cannot grasp.

Finally, this general predisposition to a poetic apprehension of urgent climactic process leads in the Prophets to what amounts to a radically new view of history. Without implying that we should reduce all thinking to principles of poetics, I would nevertheless suggest that there is a particular momentum in ancient Hebrew poetry that helps impel the poets toward rather special construals of their historical circumstances. If a prophet wants to make vivid in verse a process of impending disaster, even, let us say, with the limited conscious aim of bringing his complacent and wayward audience to its senses, the intensifying logic of his medium may lead him to statements of an ultimate and cosmic character. Thus Jeremiah, imagining the havoc an invading Babylonian army will wreak:

> *I see the earth, and, look, chaos and void,*
> *the heavens—their light is gone.*
> *I see the mountains, and, look, they quake,*
> *and all the hills shudder. (Jer. 4:23–24)*

He goes on in the same vein, continuing to draw on the language of Genesis to evoke a dismaying world where creation itself has been reversed.

A similar process is at work in the various prophecies of consolation of Amos, Jeremiah, Ezekiel, Isaiah: national restoration—in the development from literal to hyperbolic, from fact to fantastic elaboration, that is intrinsic to biblical poetry—is not just a return from exile or the reestablishment of political autonomy but a blossoming of the desert, a straightening out of all that is crooked, a wonderful fusion of seedtime and reaping, a perfect peace in which calf and lion dwell together and a little child leads them. Perhaps the Prophets might have begun to move in approximately this direction even if they had worked out their message in prose, but I think it is analytically demonstrable that the impetus of their poetic medium reinforced and in some ways directed the scope and extremity of their vision. The matrix, then, of both the apocalyptic imagination and the messianic vision of redemption may well be the distinctive structure of ancient Hebrew verse. This would be the most historically fateful illustration of a fundamental rule bearing on form and meaning in the Bible. We need to read this poetry well because it is not merely a means of heightening or dramatizing the religious perceptions of the biblical writers—it is the dynamic shaping instrument through which those perceptions discovered their immanent truth.

CHAPTER 9

Scripture and
Culture

A great deal has changed in this country since that distant era of origins when the Pilgrim founders habitually thought of America as the New Israel. But even at this late date in the process of secularization, many of the ambiguities of our cultural predicament are still linked to the long aftermath of a culture centered on the Bible.

In order to do any justice to this historical phenomenon, we have to shuttle back and forth between two different, if overlapping, meanings of the term *culture*—the prestige sense of the word, which involves serious literature, music, art, and philosophy; and the anthropological sense, which addresses itself to the characteristic patterns of behavior of ordinary people in quotidian and ritual situations. With regard to the persisting cultural presence of the Bible, there is often a causal connection between culture in the anthropological and culture in the prestige sense: the novels of Melville are a repeated argument with and recasting of the Bible, but that could scarcely have come about had not Bible reading and Bible quoting been so pervasive in the American home of the earlier nineteenth century.

It is sometimes claimed that the historical criticism of the Bible, an enterprise that can be taken back as far as Spinoza but that first reached full momentum in nineteenth-century Germany, is responsible for the erosion of the authority of the Bible. The facts of the matter seem to me more complicated than that. Many of the major figures in biblical criticism have been believers and even clerics, and their project has been not to deny the truth of the Bible but to change the terms in which that truth is conceived. This general point has been argued cogently by Hans W. Frei in his seminal study *The Eclipse of Biblical Narrative* (1974):

> In effect, the realistic or history-like quality of biblical narratives, acknowledged by all, instead of being examined for the bearing it had in its own right on meaning and interpretation, was immediately transposed into the quite different issue of whether or not the realistic narrative was historical.[1]

Before the dawn of modernity, the biblical text, in both Christian and Jewish traditions, was variously but vigorously construed as revealed truth—divinely underwritten in every detail, every particle and letter. When the emergence of a new historical perspective in the understanding of the past made this view of the Bible increasingly difficult to maintain, there came about what Frei calls a "simple transposition and logical confusion between two categories or contexts of meaning and interpretation"—that is, between what is history-like and what is actually historical in the Bible. As part of the project, moreover, of penetrating to the historical kernel, scholars adopted the new tools of philology to question the integrity of the sundry biblical texts. Where for the imagination of the believer there had been one Bible, majestically unfolding step by step from "In the beginning God created . . ." onward, there was now a welter of E, J, P, and D documents, scribal glosses, editorial bridges, redactional revisions, shards and fragments pasted together from a hundred conjectured ancient sources.

It may seem self-evident that this whole enterprise should undercut the possibility of belief in Scripture as the word of the living God, and in fact the nineteenth century in particular offers numerous instances of intellectuals who suffered an irreversible loss of faith through the corrosive effect of biblical criticism. It should be stressed, though, that biblical criticism, however skeptical, however revisionist, however atomistic in its approach to the text, has also represented an effort to get at the truth behind the text. In many respects this resembles any modern scholarly investigation of a corpus of ancient documents—but not, I would argue, in one respect. It is as if the biblical scholar were saying, In all good intellectual conscience, I must concede that these words, in the order and form that have been passed down to us, are not literally the words of the eternal God, but if only I could analyze them finely enough, match them with enough archaeological evidence and extrabiblical documents, perhaps I could begin to glimpse the originating truth, the hidden historical core of those epoch-making doctrines and values that have determined the lives of so many millions these past two thousand years. In this regard, modern biblical scholarship is the particularly urgent turn given by revealed religion to the quest for origins initiated by European romanticism.

Let me offer a contemporary American instance of how this attitude percolates down from the high culture of esoteric scholarship to more popular strata. A few years ago, an enterprising editor named Hershel Shanks created a glossy, stylish, illustrated bimonthly magazine called *Biblical Archaeology*

Review. The magazine runs brief, informative articles, accompanied with sumptuous color photographs, by reputable archaeologists and biblical scholars on particular excavations, on newly discovered inscriptions or documents, on ancient Near Eastern cultic practices, and so forth. The *Biblical Archaeology Review* has more than 125,000 subscribers, a figure I find astounding. To judge by the letters to the editor and by the advertisements, many if not most of this group are believing Christians—though not, it is safe to assume, unswerving fundamentalists.

There is clearly something in all this beyond a mere fad of archaeology. If I try to imagine what tens of thousands of believing Christians (and Jews as well) are up to reading a magazine like *Biblical Archaeology Review,* I am led to conclude that they are impelled by a motive similar to that of classical biblical scholarship: to know, for example, exactly how Jesus' cross was really constructed, what was the design of King Hezekiah's fortifications, what precisely were the scope and function of the practice of child sacrifice against which the Bible inveighed—in general, how did all these things *look* (hence the importance of the photographs); and, through all this material knowledge, to get back to the core of historical truth from which the Bible issued. What is involved here, as I have suggested, is more than a fascination with the archaic: one does not find magazines on pre-Columbian or Greco-Roman archaeology with this many subscribers, and it is hard to imagine how the investigation of other regions could have the peculiar spiritual urgency that these inquiries into biblical antiquity have for Jewish and Christian readers.

I have dwelled on this example because it strongly suggests that the historical criticism of the Bible, though it is often thought of as a secularization of Scripture, might better be described as an attempt to recover the religious truth of the Bible through means of investigation compatible with secular categories. Since this is hardly an activity for fundamentalists, it is by no means a question of trying to "prove" the validity of the Bible through secular means but rather one of adducing visual evidence for the concrete realities of biblical experience, even when they are camouflaged, distorted, or at best barely glimpsed in the verbal formulations of the received text. I would contend not that biblical criticism has been bent on unseating the Bible from its authoritative role but rather that its effort to get at the truth of the Bible has been directed by what A. N. Whitehead, in a different but related context of intellectual history, called "misplaced concreteness." It is, I would grant, intriguing to see in an Assyrian bas-relief the exact design of the siege weapons used against the Judaean city of Lachish, and perhaps this may clarify an obscure phrase in Isaiah or a biblical account of a military campaign. But bridging the gap between our material world and that of ancient Israel does not close the existential distance between modern people and ancient text, does not provide access to the complex spiritual truths of the texts.

Since we live in the aftermath of a biblically centered culture, attitudes toward the Bible are often still an index of more general ideological positions. But before I try to sketch out any of these correlations, I would observe that when we move from culture in the prestige sense to popular culture, the decentering of the Bible may have to do much less with conscious attitude than with a simple erosion of connection. In the broad movement of secularization, which biblical criticism intersects at a somewhat oblique angle, people in large numbers long ago stopped reading the Bible; for millions, the peripherality of the Bible is a matter not of skepticism but of ignorance. Any teacher of literature will be familiar with the problem Northrop Frye touches on in the introduction to his book *The Great Code*—that many manifestations of the Western literary tradition, because they are formulated in terms of biblical imagery, biblical plots, specific verses from the Bible, have become unintelligible to contemporary readers.[2]

My impression is that the Bible has fared worse in this regard than the Greek and Latin classics that constitute the other matrix of Western literature. It is true that very few secondary-school students actually learn Greek any more, but most of those who go on to college have read the *Odyssey* in translation, or at any rate encounter it in the first couple of years at college; as a result, they are likely to have some context for the allusions to Homer in Joyce's *Ulysses,* but none at all for the allusions to the Elijah story in the same novel, the Book of Kings by this time having become the kind of text most people have heard of but never glanced at. It may be that this endemic illiteracy in relation to the Bible is by now beyond remedy, though perhaps the catastrophe might at least be mitigated by trying to learn in an academic setting how to read the Bible as a body of compelling literary texts instead of merely *investigating* Scripture. This is a point to which I will return.

Given the twin erosion of plain knowledge of the Bible and of belief in the Bible as divinely revealed truth, the notion that the Bible has real prescriptive authority in governing our moral and political lives would seem to be restricted to fundamentalist groups. There are, of course, substantial numbers of nonfundamentalist Christians and Jews who try to take the Bible seriously, but in most instances they would ultimately fail the test of according prescriptive authority to Scripture. One readily sees this whenever there is an unambiguous conflict between contemporary mores, especially those deemed progressive, and explicitly stated biblical values. Thus, the biblical view of homosexuality leaves little latitude for interpretation: it is an abomination to the Lord, a practice associated with the hateful corruption, both sexual and cultic, of the surrounding pagan world from which Israel must distance

itself. Christian fundamentalists have been vocal in respond-
ing to the prescriptive force of biblical statements on this
issue; in more "advanced" Christian and Jewish circles, however, where homosexual clergymen and congregations have
gained acceptance, it is clear that the real prescriptive force
comes from contemporary attitudes rather than from
Scripture. My observation is not intended to suggest that we
should aspire to a return of Scripture as prescription but only
to locate a significant cultural shift in the source of authority.

If the Bible, then, has ceased to be literally authoritative for
the majority of Americans, it nevertheless remains associated
with the idea of authority. America has never been an authori-
tarian society, but it has by and large respected the idea of
authority. Its leaders, for better or for worse, have often been
reassuring father figures; it has honored written traditions,
religious and secular, as well as traditional institutions; even
in its most extravagant expressions of individualism, it has
assumed that there is a fundamental difference between freedom and anarchy. The turmoil of the late 1960s created an
alternative to this set of assumptions by introducing into
American political consciousness, without the support of an
articulated ideology of anarchism, the idea that authority as
such was the real enemy. The one political bumper sticker
that (in California, at least) has survived twenty years of ideological changes is the two-word injunction QUESTION
AUTHORITY.

In our culture, whether we call it Judeo-Christian or post-
Judeo-Christian, the first textual association with the idea of
authority is the Bible. You can bet that the man or woman at
the wheel of the car whose bumper enjoins us to question all
authority will be among the first to consign Deuteronomy and
Matthew to the dustheap of discarded instruments of oppres-
sion. The new fundamentalism can be seen as an equal and
opposite response to this impulse of rejection, the allure of

authority turning into a flirtation with authoritarianism and the idea of authoritative Scripture being transformed into a literalist attribution of absolute authority to every jot and tittle of the biblical text.

Some of the current controversies in literary studies in this country vividly illustrate how certain lines of relation to the Bible readily extend into other areas and help determine underlying political attitudes. Of late, a great deal has been said, by feminists, Marxists, deconstructionists in particular, about the "canon" of literary works and how it is inevitably determined by suspect ideological considerations. Canon, we should recall, is a concept drawn from the history of the institutional reception of the Bible, and it can be applied to a large and highly heterogeneous body of poetic, fictional, and dramatic texts only by way of loose analogy. Its current use, then, involves a degree of polemical distortion, suggesting that there is in literary tradition a kind of hidden equivalent of the formal councils of ecclesiastical authorities who decide on principles of inclusion and exclusion, and that the status of the noncanonical literary text is fixed and absolute, like an apocryphal work excluded by the rabbis or church fathers and deemed forever outside the scriptural pale.

American literary scholars touched by the doctrines of deconstruction have been particularly vocal in raising suspicions about existing canons and arguing for the unsettling of canons. With their notion that all hierarchical oppositions in texts are reversible, that the peripheral can become central, outside can become inside (or, as one would say more biblically, that the last will be first), the supplanting of the literary canon has been very much a political slogan. One of the most prominent advocates of this program of deconstruction in the last few years has been Jonathan Culler. Politically, Culler is a product of the SDS of the 1960s who has settled in comfortably as a successful member of the academy at an Ivy League institution, carrying the banner of deconstruction as his own equivalent of the QUESTION AUTHORITY bumper sticker, and of late channeling the revolutionary impulse of his early years into a strident version of feminism.

It is instructive, then, that Culler, whose own work is limited to the nineteenth and twentieth centuries and, except for an early book on Flaubert, deals with theoretical rather than with literary works, should have expressed outrage that the September 1984 meeting of the English Institute chose to devote a whole set of papers to the literature of the Hebrew Bible. One might have thought that such a programming decision would have been a matter of indifference to a scholar of Culler's interests, but instead he construed it as a kind of betrayal of the trust of literary studies. The sense of betrayal for Culler was no doubt sharpened by the fact that the organizer of the English Institute session on the Bible was none other than Geoffrey Hartman, the senior figure in the small group of prominent scholars at Yale who have been responsible for putting deconstruction on the American academic map.

Now, Culler formulated his objections as a kind of intellectual church-state issue, arguing that the enterprise of literary studies was fundamentally secular, committed to the critical spirit of secularity, and that therefore it had no business dealing with texts and topics that were the domain of benighted creedal interests. This definition of the literary in contradistinction to the scriptural as an opposition between secular and religious will not stand much scrutiny. Many of the major works of the Western literary tradition, even if we refrain from calling it a canon, are profoundly religious in character, from Dante to Milton to Dostoevski to T. S. Eliot, and many writers, like John Donne and W. H. Auden, have produced both secular and religious texts linked by complex affinities. To suggest that the religious dimension of such works is not the concern of literary scholars makes no more sense than proposing that the psychological dimension of literary texts should be left solely to the psychologist. I would add that on the scriptural side, there are elements of the biblical texts that are intrinsically secular—witness the Song of Songs, Ecclesiastes, and much of the Book of Proverbs—however later tradition reinterprets them religiously, and so here, too, the secular-religious opposition collapses.

The real reason, it seems to me, that the introduction of the Bible should be anathema to the radical deconstructionist is the specter of authority that the Bible evokes. Here is the very source and fount of the concept of binding canon smuggled into the realm where progressive spirits are fighting the good fight to break down the barriers of canon, displace major with minor, and let in the excluded from below and beyond.

To insist, as I have done, on an association of ideas in our culture between Scripture and authority is to beg the more essential question of whether Scripture still has any authority. One obvious answer would be a kind of tautology: that Scripture has authority for those who continue to believe, whether as fundamentalists or in some revisionist fashion, that it is the revealed word of God. Such belief, for many Americans, may be translated into political motives as diverse as a dedication to pursue justice and mercy in social policy or an opposition to the teaching of evolutionary theory in public schools; in any case, the authority of the biblical text is strong enough to compel action.

This self-evident answer to the question of the authority of Scripture is worth mentioning because it suggests that, however skeptical a secular observer may choose to be, the imperative presence of the Bible remains something serious to conjure with in contemporary American life. Polls actually indicate that well over 80 percent of all Americans still claim to believe in the Bible as revealed truth. Nevertheless, there is a large group of Americans who are not inclined to attribute a divine source to Scripture; some of these are conscious secularists, others what could be called casual nonreligionists, and still others adherents to some post-traditional form of Judaism or Christianity. It might at first appear that for this sizable group the answer to the question about the continuing authority of Scripture should be an unequivocal no. In fact, I think our cultural situation vis-à-vis the Bible is more interestingly ambiguous than would be allowed for by a neat division into believers and nonbelievers.

Let me try to illustrate this ambiguity by describing the double-edged thrust of an activity in which I have been personally involved over the past fifteen years, the attempt to fashion a new literary approach to the Bible. When I wrote my first essay on this subject, in 1975,[3] decrying the concentration of a century of biblical scholarship on purely excavative issues and calling for intellectually rigorous literary perspectives, I fancied, rather ignorantly, that I was a voice crying out in the wilderness. As I soon discovered, a whole new generation of biblical scholars in this country was beginning to turn, perhaps a little falteringly, from the search for Ugaritic loanwords and the determination of the historicity of the texts to considerations of literary art. Since the mid-1970s a spate of articles and books on the Bible with literary emphases has appeared, and in the last few years, predictably, there have also been a few signs of backlash, which, however, by no means impedes the continuing forward rush of the literary trend in biblical studies.

All this is clearly beginning to make a difference in how the Bible is thought about and taught in American seminaries, colleges, and universities. Intriguing methodological issues are involved in this shift, but beyond methodology, what is at stake is a pursuit in the Bible of a different order of truth—to invoke again Hans Frei's terms, it is a turning from the truth of history to the truth of realism, that is, to what may not be a factual account of events but is coherently history-like.

What effect does this adoption of literary perspectives have on the authority of Scripture? In my view, the effect is, necessarily, a paradoxical one. To read the Bible with literary eyes would seem to complete a long process of secularizing Scripture, and hence of undercutting any claim it might have to authority. On another level (or perhaps one should say, for other minds), the literary reading of the Bible provides a means of getting in touch again with the religious power of Scripture and so reinstates scriptural authority in new terms. The undercutting of authority is obvious enough; the way in which it is reinstated may need more detailed explanation.

Although the category of literature, as I have said, cuts across both religious and secular experience, our cultural operating assumption is that the source of literary works, however profound or intricate they may seem, is human. In Anglo-American culture, certain attempts have been made, beginning with Matthew Arnold, to instate literature as a kind of substitute religion in reaction to a general waning of faith. But these efforts have not fared well, and their ultimate devolution is reflected in the tendency of many literary theorists today to deny the privileged status and the very distinctiveness of literary discourse, putting the plays of Shakespeare on a level with menus, graffiti, and bureaucratic directives. We need not accede to such polemical simplifications, but the fact remains that when we analyze, say, exalted poetry like Keats's odes, we are quite conscious that it is a particular human mind, working through a complex interplay of linguistic phenomena, semiotic codes, and literary conventions, that is responsible for the beauty of the poems. When these same instruments of analysis are directed toward Psalms or the Song of the Songs or the poetry of Isaiah, it would seem inevitable that texts defined by tradition as sacred Scripture will be seen as human productions.

Literary appreciation does not automatically contradict belief in the inspired character of the text, but it can manage quite comfortably without reference to such belief. Recently, after a public lecture I delivered on biblical narrative, a young man wearing the small knit skullcap and trimmed beard of modern Jewish Orthodoxy asked me whether the complexities of moral motivation in the story I had discussed were not evidence of the divine inspiration that had produced the story. I was obliged to respond that, unfortunately, no literary analysis could confirm faith in this way and that certain gifted writers, including thorough secularists like Henry James and Joseph Conrad as well as intent monotheists like the authors of Genesis and the David story, manifested this ability to imagine moral dilemmas and ambiguities of motivation with an uncanny complexity.

But if it is true that a literary approach to Scripture in no way implies that the biblical text has a uniquely privileged status, my Orthodox questioner was right in one respect. The historical criticism of the Bible is rooted in a view of truth associated with nineteenth-century positivism that does not sit well with any sense of the moral or spiritual authority of Scripture. In this view, what counts is what really happened once in the coordinates of earthly time and space, what can be uncovered with the archaeologist's spade, measured by carbon dating, or at least inferentially determined as the actual material cause behind the elaborate layers of verbal mediation that constitute the biblical text. Literary analysis, on the other hand, brackets the question of history, not necessarily out of indifference to history but because it assumes that factual history is not the primary concern of the text and that it is, in any case, largely indeterminable, given the scant data we have to work with at a remove of two to three millennia from the originating events to which the text refers.

A literary approach, instead, directs attention to the moral, psychological, political, and spiritual realism of the biblical texts, which is a way of opening ourselves to something that deserves to be called their authority, whether we attribute that authority solely to the power of the human imagination or to a transcendent source of illumination that kindled the imagination of the writers to express itself through these particular literary means. The oft-quoted rabbinical dictum *dibra torah kilshon benei 'adam*, "The Torah spoke in human language," must be applied not merely to the idioms of Scripture but to the adoption by the biblical writers of an elaborate set of literary instruments for the articulation—perhaps, indeed, for the discovery—of their religious vision. Ethical monotheism was delivered to the world not as a series of abstract principles but in cunningly wrought narratives, poetry, parables, and orations, in an intricate patterning of symbolic language and rhetoric that extends even to the genealogical tables and the laws. We will scarcely feel the forceful modulations with which the texts address us unless we somehow attend to the literary forms of the address.

The difference between the project of the new literary criticism of the Bible and that of modern historical criticism may be usefully conceived as a closing of distance between reader and text versus an interposition of distance between reader and text. Although the historical critic may regard the religious character of the text with the utmost seriousness, his method implies an underlying view of the text as an inert object of investigation—the stratified verbal deposits of the life of ancient Israel that need to be carefully gauged, discriminated, and classified so that we can build hypotheses about both the evolution of the text and the life behind the text. What is tacitly assumed, though rarely admitted, is a vantage point of cognitive superiority from which the modern investigator overviews the ancient text, and that assumption of superiority entails a sense of existential distance from the text.

By contrast, the literary analyst, though he should certainly be aware of the differences of ancient mind-set and ancient literary procedures, presupposes a deep continuity of human experience that makes the concerns of the ancient text directly accessible to him. These millennia-old expressions of fear, anguish, passion, perplexity, and exultation speak to us because they issue from human predicaments in some respects quite like our own and are cast in the molds of plot, character, dialogue, scene, imagery, wordplay, and sound play that are recognizable analogues to the modalities of literary texts more easily familiar to us, closer to us in time and space.

Let me try to bring the argument into sharper focus through an illustration of how historical criticism and literary criticism respectively read a biblical text. Genesis 33 reports the reunion of Jacob and Esau after twenty years. Jacob, one recalls, has fled to his uncle Laban in Mesopotamia in fear for his life after having deceived his blind father by stealing the blessing meant for Esau. When he returns, loaded with wives and concubines and sons and cattle, he is still fearful of what Esau might do. On the night before the meeting, he wrestles in the dark with the mysterious stranger who at daybreak confers on him the numinous name of Israel. When the brothers finally meet, Esau rushes up to Jacob and embraces him, and the two at last are reconciled.

What ought to be attended to in such a text? For the late E. A. Speiser, whose commentary on Genesis in the Anchor Bible series is one of the American monuments to the documentary approach to the Pentateuch, there is scarcely any hesitation about emphasis. Given only a page to devote to the episode, he makes a couple of brief and very general remarks about the "affectionate reunion" of the brothers and then proceeds to more serious business:

The sympathetic portrayal of Esau accords well with the picture that *J* drew of him in ch. xxvii. The present account of the meeting is largely from the same hand, perhaps even entirely. To be sure, vss. 5, 10, and 11 use the term Elohim, hence many critics would assign all or most of 4–11 to *E*. Actually, however, the argument is far from conclusive.[4]

And with this Speiser goes on to consider in detail why the passage is not necessarily a composite but may be plausibly attributed to J, with a little appendix from P in the last four verses of the chapter.

I am concerned here not with whether Speiser is right or wrong or with the methodological problems in making these discriminations about different sources in the biblical text but rather with the relation to the text in which this kind of analysis places us. The encounter between Jacob and Esau, surely one of the great surprising climaxes of the patriarchal narratives, is dismissed with a perfunctory gesture of appreciation. The force and significance of the imagined scene are assumed to be self-evident, hardly requiring any minute analysis— though in fact what this meeting means to each of the brothers is far from obvious, and the theme of lordship and subservience that has followed the story of the brothers from the womb is reasserted here with fascinating ironic complications. For the documentary critic, however, the real concern is not the imaginative coherence of the narrative invention—Frei's "realism"—but the historical mediation of the text. Thus, in Speiser's commentary it is not Jacob and Esau but E, J, and P who become the subject of investigation. In this way the text is held at a distance for inspection, and any voice that might speak from its imagined situation to our actual one is in effect suppressed.

This is not the place to launch a close reading of the whole complex episode, but I would like to comment briefly on two features of the reunion in order to suggest the kind of questions a literary analysis might raise and what that might have to do with a perception of the authority of the text. From the beginning of the tale of the twins, as I have intimated, what has been explicitly at stake is who will be lord (*'adon*) and who will be servant (*'eved*). The opposition is first set out in the oracle to the pregnant Rebekah: "One nation will be stronger than the other, / and the elder will serve [*ya'avod*] the younger" (Gen. 25:23). The reversal of primogeniture announced in the oracle is certainly unambiguous, and this reversal would seem to be irrevocably confirmed first in the selling of the birthright to Jacob and then, still more clearly, when Jacob steals their father's blessing and Isaac must tell the outraged Esau, "Look, I have made him master over you, and all his brothers I have given him as servants . . ." (Gen. 27:37).

What is curious about the reunion of the brothers in Genesis 33, which is, by the way, also the last reported meeting between them in the biblical record, is that it has a look of disconfirming what has been so abundantly confirmed. Esau repeatedly addresses Jacob directly in a fraternal second-person singular, but only once, in the middle of the dialogue (verses 10–11), does Jacob use the second-person form—and this immediately after Esau has called him "my brother." Otherwise, Jacob, after having approached Esau by prostrating himself seven times, maintains the deferential third-person form of address, again and again referring to himself as "your servant" (*'avdekha*) and to Esau as "my lord" (*'adoni*), "my lord" being the very last word he says to Esau when they part.

The irony of this reversal of a reversal, this transposition of the terms of Isaac's blessing, is a rich one because there is no simple way to resolve it. Jacob's great show of subservience is, of course, a matter of prudence, as he is afraid of what Esau may do to him. Is there a moral or even political theme here, suggesting that in the ambiguous play of events true lordship is sometimes achieved by ignoring the outward trappings of superiority, perhaps by a willingness to suffer self-abasement? Or is Jacob's case for lordship somehow undercut by this behavior vis-à-vis the generous and lordly Esau? Might this final encounter between the brothers, where Jacob is servant and Esau is lord, intimate that in the uncertain medium of history there could be an element of permanent instability, unpredictability, in the seemingly clear-cut terms of the oracle and the blessing?

The irony of the scene is brought to a sharp point by Jacob's use of a single brief phrase that echoes an exchange at which he was not present, the dialogue between Isaac and the frustrated Esau in Genesis 27. For when Jacob here finally brings himself to address his brother in the second person, he says, "Please *take my blessing* that has been brought for you" (Gen. 33:11). Now, the term for blessing, *berakhah*, also means "gift," and that is obviously the sense in which Jacob is using it here. The writer chooses this term (there are at least three other common biblical words that mean "gift") because through it Jacob is made to reverse what Isaac said twenty years earlier to Esau, "Your brother came in deceit and he *took your blessing*" (Gen. 27:35), and what Esau bitterly confirmed, "And look, now he has *taken my blessing*" (Gen. 27:36).

As with the surrounding irony of the terms *lord* and *servant*, this irony leaves us poised between competing possibilities of interpretation. Are we to perceive an act of symmetrical restitution when Jacob asks Esau to take his *berakhah* just as he has taken Esau's *berakhah*? Or is this meager compensation on Jacob's part, a mere material gift (*berakhah*) offered in exchange for a stolen blessing (*berakhah*) whose benefits are permanent and untransferable? Does the pun make Jacob the unwitting target of authorial irony, perhaps suggesting that he has achieved his victory by dubious means, or is he himself aware that his choice of words reflects a reversal of his own earlier act as he now seeks to right the old wrong?

The terms of analysis I have proposed do not differ essentially from those that would be used to define the complex mimetic art of a scene from *The Red and the Black, Anna Karenina,* or *Ulysses.* The difference is a matter not of method but of context. The biblical text, that is, carries after it a wake of canonicity, not only for the believer but for the half-believer and the nonbeliever as well. One critic of the new wave of literary interest in the Bible, speaking on behalf of a latter-day piety, has protested that, after all, Jacob and Joseph are not fictional characters but rather our forefathers, the founding figures of God's covenanted people.[5] The real point, I think, is that they are both at once, and that double identity is the source of their special authority, even for the reader who is not prepared to refer them to the category of revelation.

Jacob is not merely a fictional construct, an imaginative hypothesis with the suasive force of verisimilitude. He is abundantly that, but he is also the eponymous founder of Israel, which both as physical entity and theological concept has had and continues to have enormous consequences in countless lives. The fine complexity, then, with which he is rendered in this initiating text addresses itself to our political, moral, and religious predicaments with an urgency not entirely shared by more secular fictions. The authority of the fictional imagination, as it speaks from the canonical text, assumes a cultural and a spiritual force.

The case of literary approaches to Scripture strikes me as an instructive one because it exposes so vividly the uncertain zone of aftermath in which our culture stands vis-à-vis the Bible. It may be only for a minority that Scripture remains unambiguously authoritative, yet most of us continue to feel the pressure of authority exerted by this extraordinary collection of ancient writings. From the humanist perspective, and, indeed, from many religious perspectives as well, Scripture no longer speaks in one clearly prescriptive voice, but its resonances still carry into the recesses of our spiritual and political imagination. The Bible has been a central force of coherence and continuity in our culture, and so it may not be, after all, surprising that many are now impelled to discover how they might close the gap that modernity has interposed between themselves and the biblical texts. The Bible, as I have tried to show throughout this volume, is literature before it is anything else, and so to read it "as literature" really means to *read* it again—in its compelling immediacy, in the momentum of its complex continuities. That process of reading, full of challenges and discoveries, long ago helped shape our collective lives, and it may still have a vital task to perform.

NOTES

Chapter 1: A Peculiar Literature

1. Seymour Chatman, however, has pointed out that there is a whole line of Western artworks that are essentially collaborative, where there is "authorship by committee." But even in the most extreme case, the Hollywood film where four or five people with different agendas may be responsible for the final product, audiences construct an "implied author" to whom they attribute the whole. See Chatman, *Coming to Terms: The Rhetoric of Narrative in Fiction and Film* (Ithaca: Cornell University Press, 1990), pp. 90–97.

2. David Damrosch, *The Narrative Covenant: Transformations of Genre in the Growth of Biblical Literature* (San Francisco: Harper & Row, 1987), pp. 324, 325.

3. Gabriel Josipovici, *The Book of God: A Response to the Bible* (New Haven: Yale University Press, 1988), pp. 14–15.

4. Daniel Boyarin, "The Places of Reading in Ancient Israel and Medieval Europe," *The Ethnography of Reading*, ed. Jonathan Boyarin (forthcoming).

5. Robert Alter, *The Art of Biblical Narrative* (New York: Basic Books, 1981), pp. 117–22.

6. Ibid., p. 89.

7. Robert Polzin, *Samuel and the Deuteronomist: A Literary Study of the Deuteronomic History, Part Two: 1 Samuel* (San Francisco: Harper & Row, 1989), p. 105.

8. P. Kyle McCarter, Jr., *1 Samuel* (Garden City, N.Y.: Doubleday, 1980), pp. 328, 330.

9. J. P. Fokkelman, *Narrative Art and Poetry in the Books of Samuel*, vol. 2 (Assen/Maastricht: Van Gorcum, 1986), p. 280.

10. Josipovici, *Book of God*, p. 293.

Chapter 2: Biblical Imperatives and Literary Play

1. Gabriel Josipovici, *The Book of God* (New Haven: Yale University Press, 1988), p. 300.

2. Harry Levin, *The Gates of Horn: A Study of Five French Realists* (New York: Oxford University Press, 1963), chap. 2. Gary Saul Morson, in his recent *Hidden in Plain View: Narrative and Creative Potential in "War and Peace"* (Stanford: Stanford University Press, 1987), chap. 1, makes a related point—that Tolstoy's aim was nothing less than the radical subversion through fiction of both historiography and novelistic narrative in the interests of what he considered the truth.

3. The relevant volumes are Robert Alter, *The Art of Biblical Narrative* (New York: Basic Books, 1981); Meir Sternberg, *The Poetics of Biblical Narrative: Ideological Literature and the Drama of Reading* (Bloomington: Indiana University Press, 1985); Northrop Frye, *The Great Code: The Bible and Literature* (New York: Harcourt Brace Jovanovich, 1982); and David Damrosch, *The Narrative Covenant* (San Francisco: Harper & Row, 1987).

4. Harold Fisch, *Poetry with a Purpose: Biblical Poetics and Interpretation* (Bloomington: Indiana University Press, 1988).

5. Ibid., p. 78.

6. Ibid., p. 149.

7. Ibid., p. 77.

8. Ibid., p. 12.

9. See Alter, *Art of Biblical Narrative;* George W. Savran, *Telling and Retelling: Quotation in Biblical Narrative* (Bloomington: Indiana University Press, 1988); and Sternberg, *Poetics of Biblical Narrative.*

10. Robert Alter, *The Pleasures of Reading in an Ideological Age* (New York: Simon & Schuster, 1989), p. 81.

11. Leo Lowenthal, "Sociology of Literature in Retrospect," in *An Unmastered Past: The Autobiographical Reflections of Leo Lowenthal* (Berkeley: University of California Press, 1987), p. 171.

Chapter 3: The Literary Character of the Bible

1. Harold Bloom, "'Before Moses Was, I Am': The Original and the Belated Testaments," *Notebooks in Cultural Analysis* 1 (1984): 3.

2. For all three, see the essays on the respective biblical books in *The Literary Guide to the Bible,* ed. Robert Alter and Frank Kermode (Cambridge: Harvard University Press, 1987).

3. On the perceptibility of the verbal medium as one way of distinguishing literary from historical narratives, see Thomas G. Rosenmeyer, "History or Poetry? The Example of Herodotus," *Clio* 11 (1982): 239–59.

4. I was first alerted to the shrewd play between "head" and "captain" in the story by an astute paper presented by Nahum Sarna at the Institute for Advanced Studies in Jerusalem in 1983.

5. Erich Auerbach, *Mimesis: The Representation of Reality in Western Literature,* trans. Willard Trask (Princeton: Princeton University Press, 1953), chap. 1.

6. Meir Sternberg, *The Poetics of Biblical Narrative* (Bloomington: Indiana University Press, 1985), pp. 36–38.

7. Edmund Leach and D. Alan Aycock, *Structuralist Interpretations of Biblical Myth* (Cambridge: Cambridge University Press, 1983), p. 3.

8. Robert Polzin, *Moses and the Deuteronomist: A Literary Study of the Deuteronomic History, Part One: Deuteronomy, Joshua, Judges* (New York: Seabury Press, 1980), p. 2.

9. For a general exposition of this technique, see Robert Alter, *The*

Art of Biblical Narrative (New York: Basic Books, 1981), pp. 97–113. Many examples are also analyzed by Sternberg, *Poetics of Biblical Narrative.*

Chapter 4: Narrative Specification and the Power of the Literal

1. Frank Kermode, "The Plain Sense of Things," in *An Appetite for Poetry* (Cambridge: Harvard University Press, 1989), pp. 172–88.
2. Roland Barthes, "The Reality Effect," in *French Literary Theory Today,* ed. T. Todorov (Cambridge: Cambridge University Press, 1982), pp. 11–17.
3. Franz Kafka, *The Trial,* trans. Edwin Muir (New York: Schocken Books, 1946), p. 3.
4. Robert Polzin makes an analogous argument about the relation of the beginning of 1 Samuel to the end of 2 Kings in *Samuel and the Deuteronomist* (San Francisco: Harper & Row, 1989).
5. Harold Fisch, *Poetry with a Purpose* (Bloomington: Indiana University Press, 1988).
6. Robert Alter, *The Pleasures of Reading in an Ideological Age* (New York: Simon & Schuster, 1989), pp. 39–40.

Chapter 5: Allusion and Literary Expression

1. Laurent Jenny, "The Strategy of Form," in *French Literary Theory Today,* ed. T. Todorov (Cambridge: Cambridge University Press, 1982), p. 34.
2. David Damrosch, *The Narrative Covenant* (San Francisco: Harper & Row, 1987). A still more recent study, moving on a rather different track, Harold Fisch's *Poetry with a Purpose* (Bloomington: Indiana University Press, 1988), offers a virtuoso reading of the play of allusion in Deuteronomy 32 (see pp. 55–79).
3. For a useful general definition of literary allusion in these terms, see Ziva Ben-Porat, "The Poetics of Literary Allusion," *PTL* 1, no. 1 (January 1976): 105–28.
4. These allusions have been aptly observed by Moshe Greenberg in *Understanding Exodus* (New York: Behrman House, 1969).

5. I have discussed this in "Sodom as Nexus: The Web of Design in Biblical Narrative," *Tikkun* 1, no. 1 (May 1986): 30–38.

6. I offer a more theoretical justification for the centrality of allusion to literary expression in *The Pleasures of Reading in an Ideological Age* (New York: Simon & Schuster, 1989), chap. 4.

7. The aforementioned chapter on allusion in *The Pleasures of Reading* includes a consideration of the Rahab story that touches on some of these same points, though with the aim of illustrating the general operation of literary allusion.

8. The allusion to Exodus in this verse has been noted by David Gunn, "Joshua-Judges," in *The Literary Guide to the Bible*, ed. Robert Alter and Frank Kermode (Cambridge: Harvard University Press, 1987), pp. 111–12.

Chapter 6: Literary Criticism and the Problem of Commentary

1. *The JPS Torah Commentary: Genesis*, commentary by Nahum M. Sarna; *Leviticus*, commentary by Baruch A. Levine; and *Numbers*, commentary by Jacob Milgrom (Philadelphia: JPS, 1989).

2. I have attempted to explain how Hebrew persisted as a living language through the two millennia of Diaspora existence in *The Invention of Hebrew Prose: Modern Fiction and the Language of Realism* (Seattle: University of Washington Press, 1988).

3. Meir Sternberg, *The Poetics of Biblical Narrative* (Bloomington: Indiana University Press, 1985), pp. 36–38.

4. Ibid., pp. 484–515.

Chapter 7: The Quest for the Author

1. *The Book of J*, translated from the Hebrew by David Rosenberg and interpreted by Harold Bloom (New York: Grove Weidenfeld, 1990). The term *J* is an element of the Documentary Hypothesis, initially articulated by German Bible scholars in the nineteenth century. According to that theory, the first four books of the Pentateuch were woven together by a redactor (R) out of three distinct literary strands, which in effect represent different and in many respects competing versions of the traditional history and

law. What are assumed to be the two oldest strands (tenth and ninth centuries B.C.E.) are designated J and E after the characteristic names for the Deity each uses—*Yahweh* (in German spelled with a *J*) and *Elohim*. The third strand is thought to stem from priestly circles and hence is called P. Scholarly consensus, not without some vehement dissent, views P as later, perhaps post-Exilic (fifth century B.C.E.), possibly just before the final redaction or actually blurring into R. (The Book of Deuteronomy is considered to be an entirely different strand, D, later than either E or J but earlier than P.)

2. Richard Elliott Friedman, *Who Wrote the Bible?* (New York: Prentice-Hall, 1988).

3. Robert Polzin, *Samuel and the Deuteronomist*, pt. 2. *1 Samuel* (San Francisco: Harper & Row, 1989).

4. Leslie Brisman, *The Voice of Jacob: On the Composition of Genesis* (Bloomington and Indianapolis: Indiana University Press, 1990).

Chapter 8: The Medium of Poetry

1. James L. Kugel, *The Idea of Biblical Poetry: Parallelism and Its History* (New Haven: Yale University Press, 1981).

2. On the interplay of different elements of parallelism—semantic, rhythmic, and syntactic—see the incisive remarks of Benjamin Hrushovski in "Hebrew Prosody," in *Encyclopaedia Judaica*, vol. 13 (New York: Macmillan, 1971), pp. 1200–1202.

3. Quoted in L. A. Sonnino, *A Handbook to Sixteenth-Century Rhetoric* (London: Routledge & Kegan Paul, 1968), p. 157.

4. See, for example, Stanley Gevirtz, *Patterns in the Early Poetry of Israel* (Chicago: University of Chicago Press, 1963), pp. 15–24.

5. Claus Westermann, *Basic Forms of Prophetic Speech*, trans. H. C. White (London: Lutterworth, 1967).

Chapter 9: Scripture and Culture

1. Hans W. Frei, *The Eclipse of Biblical Narrative: A Study in Eighteenth and Nineteenth Century Hermeneutics* (New Haven: Yale University Press, 1974), p. 16.

2. See Northrop Frye, *The Great Code: The Bible and Literature* (New York: Harcourt Brace Jovanovich, 1982), p. xii.

3. "A Literary Approach to the Bible," *Commentary*, December 1975, pp. 70–77. A revised version of this essay became the first chapter of *The Art of Biblical Narrative* (New York: Basic Books, 1981).

4. E. A. Speiser, *Genesis* (Garden City, N.Y.: Doubleday, 1964), p. 260.

5. James Kugel, "On the Bible and Literary Criticism," *Prooftexts* 1 (1981): 217–36.

INDEX